Narcissistic Abuse:
Everything You Need To Know

A Road Map to Healing and Thriving

by Libby Shively McAvoy

Narcissistic Abuse : Everything You Need to Know
A Road Map to Healing and Thriving
Libby Shively McAvoy

Copyright Dancing Elephants Press Publication, Dr. Gabriella Kőrösi and Libby Shively McAvoy November 2024. @ All Rights Reserved
Written by Libby Shively McAvoy
and edited by Dr. Gabriella Kőrösi

Reviews

Dr. Gabriella Kőrösi

    I am very grateful to Libby Shively McAvoy for writing this book and allowing me the privilege to edit and review the book. Providing support for healing from a personal experience from Libby's life to information on resources to seeking help, relationship, is an essential part of life. Seeking help when we need it can be difficult. The book Everything You Need to Know About Narcissistic Abuse gives essential information on resources to seek help and tips on how to handle difficult situations. This book is a great gateway toward mental health support for those who know someone with a narcissistic personality and for all of those interested in this topic. It can be easy to get lost in a relationship and be part of manipulation. Emotions in a relationship can cloud our judgment, and we can hope for a better tomorrow. I am grateful for this book providing tips on how to get out of these situations. Thank you, Libby, for allowing me to be part of this book and this beautiful journey to witness your writing and becoming an independent author.

    Gabriella

AJ

In *Everything You Need to Know About Narcissistic Abuse*, Libby provides a comprehensive guide for individuals who have experienced emotional and psychological abuse by a narcissist. As someone who was raised by a narcissistic mother, I found myself nodding yes as Libby walks the reader through the steps of recognizing emotional manipulation, why it's so difficult to break away from the narcissistic abuse, and the process of how to handle and heal from it.

This book is ideal for those, like me, who have experienced narcissistic abuse firsthand, as well as for mental health professionals or anyone seeking to understand the dynamics of narcissistic relationships. I highly recommend this book to anyone who needs help recognizing the signs of abuse and breaking free from toxic relationships. It provides both emotional support and practical guidance, empowering readers to reclaim their lives and move forward with confidence.

~ AJ

Amanda J.

Thank you for sharing such a powerful and personal story. It takes immense strength to reflect on experiences like this and even more to share them to help others recognize the signs of abuse and manipulation. The clarity and insight you've gained from such a difficult period in your life are remarkable.

Many individuals who have been in relationships with narcissists or emotionally manipulative partners can relate deeply to your journey. Terms like gaslighting, trauma bonding, and stonewalling are often unknown until someone lives through them. Your story highlights the emotional toll and isolation that accompany these relationships, as well as the confusion caused when an abuser uses charm to sway others' opinions.

The example of the walk you shared is a poignant illustration of gaslighting—twisting reality to make you question your perception. The psychological and emotional strain of constantly second-guessing oneself can be incredibly taxing, and recognizing it is a vital step toward healing and reclaiming trust in one's intuition.

Your resilience and newfound awareness are a testament to your strength. Libby, I am confident that sharing this can be a beacon for those currently navigating similar relationships, affirming that they are not alone, and that healing and clarity are possible.

With Gratitude,
Amanda J.

Chantal Weiss,

Having in the past experienced living with this personality, with not only partners but family members too, this book spoke out loud and clear to me. I was engrossed in learning all of the intricate details of the traits, the reasons they are this way, and why it was so difficult for me to break away.

Libby, pulling from personal experience of her hell of having lived with a narcissist, delivers an extensive and penetrating guide, which outlines all of the complexities of narcissistic abuse.

She helps you recognize if you are being emotionally manipulated, and the damaging effects of the toxic behaviors of this manipulation, which are all too common with these types of people.

Libby breaks down the stages the narcissist moves through, throughout the relationship, and details the specific manipulative tactics and phrases commonly used by them. Recognizing these characteristics and dynamics empowers the victim's understanding, and validates their experience. It is all too easy to feel confused and doubt ourselves when we are trapped in this mental abuse.

Libby's approach is insightful and informative, with nicely placed affirmations and quotes to cement her knowledge and compassion.

Everything You Need to Know About Narcissistic Abuse, by Libby Shively McAvoy, is a must-read for those who need hard facts and clarification of what they are up against. Whether this is the victim or the family members who need the tools fast, and a roadmap for recovery, healing, and reclaiming a free and happy life.

Much Love,
Chantal Weiss

Dr. Mehmet Yildez,

I am honored to have been a beta reader for Everything You Need to Know About Narcissistic Abuse by

Libby Shively McAvoy.

As someone with a deep interest in mental health, I found this well-crafted and insightful book incredibly resonant.

Libby offers a profound exploration of narcissistic abuse, guiding readers through the terms and tactics—like gaslighting, stonewalling, projection, and trauma bonds—that often characterize these toxic relationships. With each chapter, readers gain a clearer understanding of how manipulation, disguised as affection, can cloud judgment and isolate them from their true sense of self.

This book goes beyond simply identifying the traits of narcissistic behavior. It empowers readers with the tools to recognize red flags and break free from abusive patterns. For anyone questioning their reality, feeling "crazy," or wondering if they are the problem, Everything You Need to Know About Narcissistic Abuse offers both the wisdom and encouragement to reclaim a life of peace, self-respect, and well-being.

Written from the heart, Libby's words resonate deeply and provide invaluable insights for anyone affected by this form of abuse. I highly recommend this book to readers interested in understanding the effects of narcissism and toxic relationships in our mental health.

~Dr. Mehmet Yildez

Deb Fiore,

I am delighted and privileged to write a review of the book, *Everything You Need to Know About Narcissistic Abuse* by Libby Shively McAvoy. It is quite clear Libby is writing not only from experience but from her heart as well. Her no-nonsense guide to the mind of a narcissist is easy to read and comprehend. There is no doubt Libby has experienced the lethal abusers of narcissism. She is not unscathed and has worked hard to recover from her toxic encounters. Libby wants to share her experience to help others.

Libby identifies the different ways abusers will prey on their victims. As a trauma therapist, I can attest to how trauma can be the result of toxic relationships. Libby explains how sometimes we mistake the trauma bond of a toxic relationship as a true bond. Then we become sucked into that world of emotional and psychological abuse. Along the way, we lose our autonomy in many important ways.

Everything You Need to Know About Narcissistic Abuse presents understandable definitions of gaslighting phrases that can happen in any toxic relationship. Besides my experience with my abused clients, I was also raised by a mother who was a master at gaslighting, I empathized with many of these phrases. You may shiver when you recognize some of them because they are too familiar, too close to home.

Gaslighting is one of the many topics explored but there is much more to this book, *Everything You Need to Know About Narcissistic Abuse*. Libby is talented and writes with heartfelt emotion to describe her personal experiences. Moreover, Libby empowers the reader to understand not only the definition of toxic relationships but also gives detailed insights on how to escape those toxic relationships.

Libby's book contains valuable information to support you in discovering ways to improve your psychological and emotional well-being. When I was younger, it took many painful years to extricate myself from my toxic family and other toxic relationships. I am safer and more healthy now but this book along with therapy would have saved me many years of anguish.

This is a wonderful accomplishment, Libby. You should be proud of all your hard work. Thank you for sharing your experiences. It takes courage to show your vulnerability. Many others will benefit from your bravery. I hope everyone's journey leads them to a place where their heart and soul feel safe.

Much love and big hugs,
Deb Fiore, LICSW, Trauma Therapist

Table of Contents

Biography of Author
    Foreword: How Dating a Narcissist Changed My Life

Part I Recognizing and Understanding Emotional & Psychological Abuse

Chapter 1: Recognizing & Understanding Emotional Manipulation
　Chapter 2: Recognize Toxic Relationships & How to Break Free
　Chapter 3: Common Phrases a Narcissist Uses
　Chapter 4: Common Gaslighting Phrases
　Chapter 5: The Damaging Effect of Passive-Aggressive Behavior
　Chapter 6: Understanding Gaslighting and its Dangerous Mental Effect
　Chapter 7: The Trail of Breadcrumbs from a Narcissist
　Chapter 8: Identifying Narcissistic Abuse
　Chapter 9: Stonewalling is a Toxic Tactic

Part II Why Breaking Free from a Narcissist is As Difficult as Breaking an Opioid Addiction

Chapter 10: Fight or Flight Mode Explained Scientifically
    Chapter 11: The Opposite of a Narcissist; Empaths and Echoists
    Chapter 12: Understanding Trauma Bond
    Chapter 13: Breaking Trauma Bond & Rebuilding Confidence
    Chapter 14: Escaping the Illusion of Love Created by a Narcissist
    Chapter 15: Understanding Reactive Abuse
    Chapter 16: The Narcissistic Epidemic and How to Battle It

Part III No Contact

Chapter 17: The Cycle of Breaking No Contact

Chapter 18: Breaking Free from the Agony of Covert Psychological Abuse

Chapter 19: Only Narcissists Defend Flying Monkeys

Chapter 20: The Psychological Effects of Narcissistic Abuse

Chapter 21: Communication With a Narcissist is Like Opening Pandora's Box

Chapter 22: The Cycle of a Narcissist

Part IV Moving on and Recognizing Healthy Relationships

Chapter 23: Recognizing an Emotionally Safe Relationship
    Chapter 24: Learning to Trust
    Chapter 25: How Can I Ever Trust Again?
    Chapter 25: Boundaries 101
    Chapter 26: Soothing a Dysregulated Nervous System

Parting Words

Libby Shively McAvoy
Biography

Libby Shively McAvoy is a Personal Development and Relationship Coach specializing in Emotional Intelligence. Having survived both physical and emotional abuse, Libby believes strongly that increasing emotional intelligence has the ability to decrease school-age bullying as well as abuse in adult years and increase personal success overall in life.

She combines her life experience, ANMAB Coaching, and 500hr Yoga Certifications for a successful career. Libby enjoys motivational speaking, leading wellness, meditation, & yoga retreats globally, writing, parenting, traveling, cooking, & seeking knowledge.

Her mission is to awaken, inspire, and empower others to stop living on autopilot and to start living the life they love. Libby is available on multiple social media sites.

www.libbyshivelymcavoy.com[1]
contact@libbyshivelymcavoy.com

---

1. http://www.libbyshivelymcavoy.com/

Foreword

When I dated a narcissist, I had never even heard of that word. I had previously been married for twenty-one years and only dated a couple of guys after my marriage ended. It is fair to say I was naive to manipulation and emotional and psychological abuse. Now that I have survived both psychological and physical abuse, I can say the red flags were clear, but when I was being manipulated, my head was in the clouds. I would read things that I could completely relate to, and that is when the lightbulb went on that I might not be crazy after all, might just be dating a narcissist. If you are dating a narcissist, but they are making you feel crazy or possibly portraying *you* as a narcissist, I hope this book provides the clarity you need to move forward with the life you deserve.

How Dating a Narcissist Changed My Life

Discovering I was in a relationship with a narcissist has changed my life. I got schooled in the most challenging way. The results were both good and bad.

The Good Things I Learned

Terms, oh my, the terms I have learned. I had never heard of narcissism, stonewalling, passive-aggressive behavior, entitlement, gaslighting, or trauma bond. Once you experience it, you learn all the terms and resonate with them. It is devastating emotionally, but at least my awareness has grown exponentially. I can now spot manipulative tactics a mile away. My intuition is more tuned in. And I will never fall for that again.

The Hardships of Dating a Narcissist

The hard part is thinking you are in love and finally, after years of psychological abuse, realizing that person was never who you thought. It was all an illusion.

Dating a narcissist makes you doubt all your thoughts. It breaks you down and makes you feel crazy. It took a hard toll on my self-esteem, and I lost friends because he isolated me. Narcissists put on the charm to outside friends and family. So, he wins their approval. Then, when he told them things about me, like I might be suicidal and was concerned about my mental health, they believed him. Meanwhile, I was fine; it was he who was making me feel crazy, isolated, and sad. He said things behind my back that I did not learn about until years later, trying to discredit my reputation.

Being gaslighted makes a person feel crazy. We were on a walk one day, and I asked if we were going the opposite way down the hill we had previously climbed. I am geographically challenged and did not know the area well. He was outraged; he said we had never been there before. Then he accused me of being with someone else, which was absurd because I spent all my time with him. Finally, after I persisted, he admitted: "he forgot." He did not forget. It was a walk we had taken two weeks prior. That is just one example.

Being with a narcissist is very lonely. You can be in the same room, and when they want to punish you, they will stop speaking to you, sometimes with their arms crossed, pouting. Stonewalling and silent treatment are highly detrimental. You can ask what they would like for dinner because you are trying to be friendly and get no response. It makes you desperate to communicate.

Passive-aggressive behavior is brutal to be around. If you have something to say, say it. Do not make someone feel like they must walk on eggshells to avoid upsetting you. My ex would often stomp around and slam doors. This is because he was unable to express his emotions so he resorted to tantrums like a young child.

Narcissists are also champions at projecting. My ex tried to make me feel like I was the Narc. But the difference is I cared enough to look up online quizzes and get examined because if I were, I would want as much help as possible. A Narcissist would never be able to admit that or seek help.

Final Thoughts

Being with a narcissist is like having your world flipped upside down and inside out. Imagine being inside of a snow globe, living in what you had dreamed and imagined to be everything you wanted, only when you arrived, it is nothing but a cold and isolated lonely place. A place where the person you love keeps shaking your world up, seeing if you keep standing up after being knocked down, and waiting for you to react so that they can blame you.

Once you learn the patterns, you understand what is going on. At that point, you can break the trauma bond by going with no contact. That is the only way out and back to your sanity.

"Hurting them back will not heal your pain." ~Author Unknown

Recognizing and Understanding Emotional Manipulation

Over the past ten years, I have learned that my mental well-being is equally as important as my physical well-being. As a yoga instructor, I talk a lot about staying balanced in body, mind, and spirit, but I somehow overlooked the importance of my soul. I managed to keep my mind decluttered and my spirits high. Meanwhile, the light of my soul was being dimmed by a manipulative relationship that I could not see.

Nearly half of all women and men in the United States will experience psychological aggression by an intimate partner in their lifetime. (Black et al, 2011)

Have you ever been emotionally manipulated?

I was in a psychologically abusive relationship for several years before I woke up and realized what was happening. It was literally sucking the life out of me. I was gaining weight, losing muscle, losing energy, crying all the time, suffering from migraines often, and losing my hair.

"A narcissist's weapon of choice is often verbal — slander, lies, playing the victim in flipped tales of who was the abuser, gossip, rage, verbal abuse, and intentional infliction of emotional pain. It is a systematic dismantling of another person's relationships, reputation, emotional, physical, and spiritual health, life, and very soul. This is why narcissists are so often called 'emotional vampires'" ~ Gail Meyers

When you are being emotionally blackmailed or manipulated, it is hard to see the signs until the obvious physical symptoms of the abusive cycle start to present themselves. Once you recognize what is happening, it is imperative for your health and well-being that you leave the relationship to protect both your heart and soul. There is no winning or resolving the situation with such an energy vampire.

An energy vampire is someone who sucks the life out of you and drains all of your energy. This term to me, best describes a narcissist. Some people will never admit or even realize how toxic they are. They will not take personal responsibility for the pain and wrongdoing they cause. Narcissists and gaslighters are soul terrorists. They use manipulation, deceit, lies, emotional blackmail, and brainwashing to control and berate you to get what they want.

Some Common Forms of Emotional Manipulation That I Experienced:

- *Shifting Goals*- moving the goalposts so that you can never achieve the criteria to satisfy them. You feel you can never say or do the right things to please them.
- *Changing the subject*- deflecting so that they can avoid the issue when their behavior is addressed
- *Gaslighting*- the person makes their victim doubt their understanding of reality to the point where they feel crazy.
- *Emotional abuse:* The person misuses emotions to manipulate others, belittling and degrading that person.
- *Passive-aggressive*- indirectly negative feelings are expressed instead of talking about it.
- *Evoking fear*- the person plays on the other person's fears to get what they want.
- *Stonewalling*- refusing to talk to your partner by giving the silent treatment.
- *Causing Reactive Anger*- provoking you to yell or act out so they can blame you.

I felt I was always walking on eggshells in that relationship, especially toward the end. I could never say or do the right thing. He would bait me in and then bash me down, creating a lot of emotional confusion, which I later learned was a trauma bond*. I was mentally and emotionally exhausted. He would justify his actions, change the subject if I was making sense in an argument, shame me, and he would even play the victim.

"At some point along the timeline of being in contact with a narcissist sociopath, many survivors will come to a place where they recognize that the toxic person provides no value to their life. Toxic people have a way of completely wearing out their welcome. It's at this point that survivors cut contact and refuse to be a pawn in the abusive game. Toxic people don't realize that survivors authentically grow weary of the ridiculousness, find recovery from the abuse, and eventually move on without looking back." ~ Shannon Thomas

Returning my soul to a peaceful state.

I had no idea how dysfunctional our relationship was until it was finally over, and I had moved on. When the tumultuous lifestyle ended, and I created stability for myself by blocking him, I found tranquility and order. It was as if I woke up from a terrible nightmare, and suddenly, the birds were serenading me, the sun was shining, and incredible peace was restored. My soul was at peace again and able to shine. I returned to eating better, working out, and feeling like myself. My hair is thick again, and I rarely get migraines.

It did not take long before someone from my past, who had asked me out many times and I had declined because I was in a relationship, returned. This time, I said yes. He instantly recognized the light of my soul and honored and cherished it. Wow, what a difference!

Understanding the difference between healthy and unhealthy relationships.

If someone is draining your energy, please honor your soul and walk away. No matter how much you think you love and care about someone, they do not love you if they are sucking the life out of you.

Someone who loves you wants you to thrive. As I have previously written, you will know when someone truly cares about you. They want to nourish your soul so you can grow into your best self. They do not manipulate you to get what they want and drain your energy.

Emotional manipulation is psychological abuse. It is equally as damaging as physical abuse. If you are constantly fighting over the same thing without resolving the issue, if you are being isolated from friends and family, if you feel you cannot do or say anything right, if you are being cut down verbally and emotionally or have to walk on eggshells, leave the relationship.

You can try counseling before leaving the relationship, but in my experience, a manipulative, toxic person typically has childhood wounds that run very deep. This does not mean that a person cannot do the work and heal, but it takes time and effort.

I learned that I could not be his crutch. He had to do the self-work. No matter how much I loved him it would never be enough, because he had to love and accept himself. He rejected my love.

Conclusion

Love, honor, and respect yourself. Be okay with being alone rather than with someone who would dim the light of your precious soul.

You are worthy. You are worthy of joy and stability. Create the life you love. When you live authentically, you will attract someone who will cherish you when the time is right. Ultimately, we attract mirrors of who we are. However, we have to be careful because narcissists prey on people who make them look good, so they go after the best of the best. Forgive yourself if you were in a manipulative relationship; close the door, block, and move forward with your beautiful life.

"People need to understand that emotional psychological, and verbal abuse is severe abuse, and it affects your health and emotional well-being. Some people get so traumatized that they develop post-traumatic stress disorder. Just because it is invisible to some, does not mean it is not severe,

even deadly. So maybe they were not hit or beat up physically, but psychologically they were beaten down, and that has severe ramifications and greatly affects a person's ability to function properly." ~ Maria Consiglio

Thank you so much for taking the time to read this. Domestic abuse is near and dear to my heart. I specialize in emotional intelligence because I believe that we build empathy, communication, and interpersonal skills and gain self-awareness by strengthening emotional intelligence skills. These skills help reduce bullying in children and abuse in adults.

References/Resources

- If you feel you are in an abusive relationship and in danger, please call The National Domestic Violence Hotline at 1-800-799-7233 or seek counseling. You are never alone.

* Black, M.C., Basile, K.C., Breiding, M.J., Smith, S.G., Walters, M.L., Merrick, M.T., Chen, J., & Stevens, M.R. (2011). The National Intimate Partner and Sexual Violence Survey (NISVS): 2010 Summary Report. Atlanta, GA: National Center for Injury Prevention and Control, Centers for Disease Control and Prevention. Retrieved from https://www.thehotline.org/stakeholders/domestic-violence-statistics/#:~:text=Almost%20half%20of%20all%20women,and%2048.8%25%2C%20respectively).

* Deborah Quinn and Sarah Fletcher (2024) sandstone care. Trauma Bonding. Definition, Stages & Recovery. Retrieved from https://www.sandstonecare.com/blog/trauma-bonding/

"You can't heal what you didn't allow yourself to feel." ~Author Unknown

Recognizing Toxic Relationships and Breaking Free

Envato Elements Purchased Image License FG4XNQLSHR

Being in a toxic relationship does not mean *you* are a bad or toxic person. Recognizing it simply means you are aware enough to see that, as a couple, you do not work well together, and you and your partner may very well bring out the worst in each other. In some cases, one partner causes toxicity; such is the case with a narcissist. In some cases, when both partners agree, they are committed to making the relationship work, they can seek professional help and resolve the problems, but in most cases, it is best to break up and move on. In any case, it is good to be educated, even if you are single so that you can spot the red flags when and if they do occur.

Seven Types of Toxic Relationships That I Have Witnessed

1. **The Abuser:** Abuse of any kind cannot and should not be tolerated. Physical abuse is straightforward. Do not allow anyone to lay a hand on

you or harm you in any way. Verbal and emotional abuse is sometimes harder to spot, but it is equally as damaging to the soul. Withholding or controlling finances is also abusive. Sexual power should not be abused in any relationship either.

2. **The Clingy/Insecure:** Someone who is always looking for compliments lacks self-confidence. This person does not have a secure attachment. Likewise, sometimes this person refuses to accept a compliment because they do not accept and love themselves. They likely have abandonment fears as well as fears of rejection. They have traits of jealousy and will be overly controlling, perhaps not at first, but it will most likely happen.

3. **The Score Keeper:** this person is overly competitive and may seem fun at first but will constantly be trying to one-up you. You will feel like you are never good enough.

4. **The Gaslighter:** Gaslighting is an emotional manipulation that causes you to question your sanity. This person will have you questioning yourself even when you know you are correct.

5. **The Liar and or Cheater:** If you know your partner is lying to friends and family, he/she is most likely also lying to you. Cheating includes emotional, physical, and also financial, which could be withholding or hiding money from you. This person is hard, if not impossible, to trust. Lying and cheating are character flaws and big red flags.

6. **The Negative Nilly:** Someone who is constantly seeing the worst-case scenario will drag you down and drain your energy. They will look for things to complain about and make you miserable.

7. **The Narcissist:** The narcissist will be very charming on the front end of the relationship; however, they are extremely manipulative, and once they feel they have you roped in they become patronizing and demanding. They tend to speak poorly of past people they were in relationships with, refuse to take the blame, need constant validation,

and belittle others. (The narcissist may display all seven types of toxic behaviors.)

"The people in your life should be a source of reducing stress, not causing more of it." ~ The Good Vibe.com

How to Recognize a Toxic Relationship

You will know you are in a toxic relationship if you continue to have the same argument with zero resolution. If your partner drains your energy, there is prolonged negativity, or he/she cuts you down. If you feel you are walking on eggshells constantly and cannot do anything right, your relationship is probably toxic. If there is passive-aggressive behavior or one person plays the victim, you are likely in a toxic relationship.

Breaking Free from a Toxic Relationship

Often, after being in a toxic relationship, especially long term, we lose our sense of autonomy. It is best to take some time and prepare mentally before leaving the relationship unless you are in imminent danger.

- Seek professional counseling or coaching
- Surround yourself with a group of positive supportive people
- Engage in new hobbies and learn to get to know yourself again
- Build your self-esteem
- Practice self-care

"Trauma bonding makes you physiologically addicted to abuse. This explains why going no contact feels like you are coming off a drug." ~ Melanie Tonia Evans

Trauma Bond

If you are in a relationship with a narcissist or someone who gaslights you, you may have a trauma bond. It can be very confusing and you may think you have the most passionate relationship of your life.

*A trauma bond is a brutal emotional attachment that is very difficult to break because it is the intermittent cycle of reinforcement of validation and love followed by abuse. Leaving a trauma-bonded relationship has been likened to someone stopping opioid drugs- it is that difficult.

The brain vacillates between pumping out oxytocin, our bonding hormone, and cortisol, our stress hormone. The instability of this chemical cocktail breeds a hurricane in your mind flooding you with confusion and frustration. Being in a trauma-bonded relationship is extremely detrimental to your well-being. It is very important to seek professional help. It will be very important to work on connecting with your higher self and also building your emotional intelligence.

- Block the contact. Have zero contact. Block all phones and social media.
- Do not look at photos.
- Make a list of all the reasons your relationship was toxic and read it daily. This will help reinforce the fact that you do not want to return to this person, no matter how tempted you may be. Also, make a list of your partner's negative character traits. This will also help reinforce why you do not want to return.
- Next, make a list of your positive character traits
- Say positive daily affirmations such as "I am strong enough to face my fears," "With each breath, I become calmer, stronger, and more confident," and "I have the power to control my thoughts and emotions."
- Spend time alone before entering another relationship

References

* Deborah Quinn and Sarah Fletcher (2024) sandstone care. Trauma Bonding. Definition, Stages & Recovery. Retrieved from https://www.sandstonecare.com/blog/trauma-bonding/

"Healing is weird. Some days, you're okay, and you're doing fine. Other days it, it still hurts like it is fresh. It's a process with no definitive time frame. You just have to keep going and know that when it is all said and done, you're going to be okay."
~Unknown Author

Common Phrases Narcissists Love to Use

Whether you have dated a narcissist in the past or are currently in a relationship with one now, you will recognize some phrases they are likely to use. If you are in a relationship with one, but perhaps questioning if they are narcissistic if they use these phrases, it is highly likely, and if they deny and refuse to look into it, it almost is an ace in the hole.

Common Phrases A Narcissist Loves to Use

1: "What about your problems?"

They will deflect attention back to you rather than accept personal responsibility.

2: "I'm sorry; what more could you possibly want from me?"

Throwing arms up in the air and stomping around, refusing to apologize. Again, playing the victim.

3: "You caused this to happen."

Projection of blame for their deplorable behavior.

4: "Why do you always bring up the past?"

Followed by their repetitive unacceptable behavior.

5: "You didn't let me finish what I was saying."

This is where they change their story, counter, and inflict more emotional abuse.

Understanding Narcissistic Abuse

Narcissists are severely emotionally stunted. Most have experienced childhood abuse or neglect. They may appear highly mentally functioning and charismatic, but they have the emotional intelligence of an angry, hurt young child.

It may seem as though the subject is over-talked, but that is because it is difficult for those who have experienced it to understand. Victims of narcissistic abuse look for answers and similarities to what they are experiencing.

A narcissist may treat you differently in front of friends and family, isolating you further. Others will not understand when you describe the psychological abuse you are going through. You will probably even question yourself, particularly after being gaslighted. *

What hurts the most is when your friends end up liking and siding with the narcissists because of their manipulation.

Final Thoughts

Until you have experienced being with a narcissist, you really cannot understand how emotionally traumatic it is. I believe that more narcissists are lurking around than are diagnosed because most are adamant that they do not have a problem. Only 5% of the population is actually diagnosed with Narcissistic Personality disorder.*

It is tough to get away from them. They get an emotional grip on you that is difficult to describe until you have experienced it. It is like trying to set silly putty out of an infant's car seat on a hot summer day; yes, *it is that frustrating.*

If you suspect you are in a relationship with a narcissist and it has been turbulent, therapy can be beneficial in keeping your self-esteem as high as possible. Keep boundaries and stand up for yourself in any relationship.

References

*Cleveland Clinic (2024) Retrieved from https://my.clevelandclinic.org/health/diseases/9742-narcissistic-personality-disorder,8/2/2023

Sherri Gordon, Very Well Mind (2023) Is Someone Gaslighting You? Learn the Warning Signs. Retrieved from https://www.verywellmind.com/is-someone-gaslighting-you-4147470

"Heal so you can hear what is being said without the filter of your wound." ~Author Unknown

Common Gaslighting Phrases Thrown Around in Relationships

Do You Know What Gaslighting Is?

Many people have experienced gaslighting without even realizing it. It is prevalent in relationships, and sometimes parents do it to their children, too. Narcissists often use it as an intentional form of manipulation, but most people do not realize they are subconsciously emotionally abusing their loved one. Gaslighting is a form of emotional abuse that causes the victim to question their sanity.*

I have experienced it myself. It left me feeling frustrated, confused, and even angry. It made me question everything I did and even what I did not do. I felt as if I could not say or do anything right.

Five Phrases You May Often Hear in Relationships That Are ExamplesOf Gaslighlighting:

1. *You are just too sensitive.*

Oh, I heard this countless times. It hurt for a couple of reasons. First, I am, in fact, a sensitive person. But what he was really doing was disregarding how I was feeling.

2. *No wonder your ex left you.*

Ouch. That is just a rude painful statement. It left me questioning everything. Should I have done things better? Maybe I missed something I was unaware of with my ex. No, no, no..... It is all a mind game.

He wants you to think that whatever you did was so bad, but he is likely projecting in reality. He refuses to take personal responsibility and will never apologize. Assess the situation, and if you did nothing wrong, then hold your head high and give the relationship some space.

3. *If you loved me, you would...*

Well, I did love him and tried implicitly to show him. It was never enough. I knew his love language and appealed to it. Not good enough. The problem was he did not love himself. Again, it was a projection. No matter how much I loved him, I could not fill that void for him.

4. You are crazy and need professional help.

You may even get labeled a narcissist. When you do not have a problem, you typically have no problem seeking help when a loved one suggests it. I was far from crazy, but he did not want to hear my logical reasoning. From there, you can confirm you are not crazy and that he is gaslighting you. He may be the one who needs therapy but will likely resist it.

5. You can't take a joke.

This phrase is terrible because it is only used when the person knows what they said was a backhanded joke; at best, that was not funny to you. It is hurtful and emotionally abusive.

Gaslighting In a Nutshell

- Minimizes your feelings
- It makes you question your memory
- Changes subject
- Conveniently forgets or denies
- Discredits you to others
- Brushes off discussions

How to Know This Is Happening to You

- If your feelings are invalidated
- If your partner's words and actions do not align
- If your partner makes you feel guilty
- If you feel you are walking on eggshells
- If your partner plays the victim
- If you question your sanity

Final Thoughts

Not all gaslighting is intentional, but it is emotionally abusive and damaging to the soul. Learn to recognize it. Set boundaries. Be aware it is happening and tell your partner because they may not be conscious of gaslighting you. Help them understand these manipulative phases and how they hurt your feelings. In parenting, gaslighting may look like blaming your child instead of asking questions to investigate what happened.

References

*The hotline.org. (2024) What is Gaslighting? Retrieved from https://www.thehotline.org/resources/what-is-gaslighting/

"We cannot selectively numb emotions, when we numb the painful emotions, we also numb the positive emotions." ~ Brene Brown

The Damaging Effect of Passive Aggressive Behavior

How to Spot and Respond to Passive Aggressiveness

Have you dated someone who is passive-aggressive? Perhaps you have a family member, friend, or co-worker who is passive-aggressive. It is a form of manipulation that can destroy relationships. Being passive-aggressive (PA) is a coward's way of expressing themselves based on deeply rooted fears.

The PA might give silent treatment to their partner, family member, co-worker, or project, or they may have a pity party. They dance around the problems at hand without resolving them, which leaves the other person feeling resentful, hurt, and confused.

Because the behavior is so damaging to the person on the receiving end, many consider it psychological or verbal abuse, which is extremely damaging to the soul.

How Emotional Intelligence Relates

Typically, the passive-aggressive person has a very difficult time processing, accepting, and expressing their emotions. This is deeply rooted in fear and accelerated by overwhelm. Subconsciously, they have not addressed their fears, many of which are from childhood or a traumatic event that left them feeling unsafe. It leaves the partner feeling like they are tip-toeing around on eggshells.

They will use this behavior to mask uncertainty, insecurities, and discomfort in situations. Some people are more sarcastic than passive-aggressive. I have come to dislike sarcasm as well, though — It is not very nice or friendly.

When the partner of the PA shares concerns, as healthy partners would, it immediately triggers a negative reaction to the PA. This negative reaction then leaves the partner feeling discarded, unheard, and lonely. It is very emotionally damaging.

According to Medical News Today, "It is a concealed form of aggression, which can make it difficult to confront."

What is Passive Aggressive Bahvior?

- Subtle digs
- Silent treatment
- Sarcasm that is similar to gaslighting
- Using knowledge to hurt the other person's feelings intentionally
- Disrespectful tone of voice
- Saying harsh things and then stating they were kidding
- Eye rolling
- Not returning texts
- Giving the cold shoulder
- Slamming stuff around or slamming doors

How to Counter Passive Aggressive Behavior

1. Pause, breathe deeply, and respond rather than react to their behavior.
2. Use "I statements" so the PA does not feel blamed or judged.
3. Engage assertively but respectfully
4. Be empathetic but to the point.
5. Maintain your boundaries

Notice Behavioral Changes

The person I dated who was passive-aggressive thought he had great communication skills when, in reality, he was unable to resolve conflict at all. He was always super stressed out and blamed everyone else (*projected*) without taking any personal responsibility. There was a complete disconnect between what he said and what he did.

Changes in behavior are a huge red flag, especially in relationships.

In the beginning of the relationship, he was very gentle, emotional, and supportive. Several months in, when he felt like I was not going anywhere, is when the passive-aggressive behavior began. I felt everything I said was wrong or would upset him. He no longer called me pet names or said good morning, and the physical affection disappeared.

Are You the Passive Aggressive One?

If you are someone who finds yourself being passive-aggressive, please realize how hurtful it is to those who care about you. Increase your self-awareness. Pay attention to how you react in different situations and also to how you are making the people around you feel. Be aware of how your loved ones respond to you. Do not say, "I'm fine" when you are not.

I watched my ex's son retreat to his room because his dad started drinking more and more and would just dig at everyone. I started spending time in my room to get away from the negativity. This was a man I deeply cared for and there was nothing I could do to help him because he was not receptive. He saw nothing wrong with his behavior.

I would urge anyone who is a PA to observe and understand their emotions. Feel it to heal it. Maybe you are unaware of some deep fears. Journal and say positive affirmations to rewire the subconscious mind. Awareness is the catalyst for change.

How to Respond to Passive Aggressive Behavior

- Recognize the behavior
- Do not let them get your goat. Rise above.

- Avoid accusations, judgment, and shame
- Set and maintain firm boundaries
- Distance yourself

Conclusion

Ultimately, passive-aggressive behavior and projection destroyed my relationship. I have no idea if he is a covert narcissist or not, and labels are not important. What is important is that he discarded my feelings while exaggerating his own importance. God forbid I ask him to do something; he would roll his eyes and say something to the effect of, "Oh wow, now I have to be told what to do." To which I would reply very simply, "I did not tell you I asked you."

Not everyone who uses passive-aggressive language and behavior does it regularly. In fact, most of us do it for a small amount of time when we are uncomfortable. My previous boyfriend was slightly passive-aggressive, but when I called him out, we both laughed. His was nowhere near as severe and downright hurtful.

My last ex's aggression slowly ramped up. He got in a fight with, and stopped talking to, his sister, with whom he was very close; he spoke badly about his good friends and turned from being supportive of my children to despising them. That was the turning point for me.

The environment in which we live should be a peaceful calm sanctuary. I have been in enough toxic relationships to know when it is time to practice self-respect and walk away. It was heartbreaking but necessary. You can lead a horse to water, but you can't make him drink so do not drive yourself crazy trying.

"Healing doesn't mean the pain never existed. It means the damage no longer controls our lives." ~ NotSalmon.com

Understanding Gaslighting and Its Dangerous Mental Effect

Photo by Photo by Philippe Mignot on Unsplash

Many people are unaware of psychological terms for abusive behavior, such as gaslighting and stonewalling. Others are aware but do not understand the meaning, so they throw around the words inaccurately. Gaslighting is mentally and emotionally damaging.

What does it mean?

Gaslighting is a psychological manipulation that causes the victim to question their sanity. The abuser questions or denies the victim's reality, confusing them and making them doubt themselves.

Narcissists commonly use gaslighting to lower their victim's self-esteem and gain control over them. But you don't have to be a narcissist to gaslight; in fact, there are some cases where it is unintentional, and I will get to that.

When gaslighting is intentionally used to manipulate someone, its effects are gradual and can be challenging to recognize. Be aware of what it looks and sounds like and stop reacting to the abuser.

The term gaslighting originated from a British play in 1938 *. It later became a film and depicted the elements of psychological gaslighting, which leaves you in a mental fog and feeling alone.

Common Gaslighting Phrases

- I never did that.
- If I'm so awful, why are you with me?
- You're so dramatic.
- You are always twisting or exaggerating things.
- Oh, calm down.
- It wasn't a big deal.
- It was just a joke.
- Oh, so this is why your other relationships didn't work.

Isolation & Confusion

The abuser will isolate you by turning friends and family against you. If the abuser is narcissistic, they may be outgoing in public with others and make a great impression. They may pull out the chair for all the ladies or pay for the tab. Suddenly you get in the car to go home, and they are a different person to you. You can't understand what is happening. You question what you did wrong or what you did to upset them.

The reality is you did nothing wrong. The abuser drained all his energy by putting on a show and has nothing left to give. But this is all part of their plan. They want you to feel like it is your fault.

Meanwhile, when you argue with the abuser or take a relationship time out, your family is disappointed in you. They wonder what *you did* to mess up a relationship with such a "great" person. You start believing your family and friends are correct and return to the abuser apologizing.

The relationship feels rocky and unstable. You feel like you are in a small boat in the ocean in large swells being circled by sharks. You are never quite sure if you are going to get Jekyll and Hyde, so to speak. If you try to explain how you feel to the abuser, you will be told you are too sensitive, and your feelings will not be validated.

Gaslighters will deny your reality. Their warmth and charm around others and criticism and anger behind closed doors leave you with emotional whiplash.

Imagine laying on the floor of the boat, shivering cold in terrible weather conditions. You don't realize what happened when you awake because you were knocked out by a huge wave. That wave is the wave of uncertainty caused by the gaslighter.

Understanding The Forms and Phases

Gaslighting comes in a couple of forms, as mentioned earlier.

> *1 Unintentional gaslighting*- although this is not common, most of us have done it at some point, so we need to be very aware to avoid repeating it. It is a form of minimizing how the other person feels. For example, if your child falls off the swing at the playground and cuts both knees, and comes screaming and crying, you might say, "calm down, sweetie, you are going to live; it is just a little blood. Let's get a Band-Aid." You did not validate your child's feelings. You might have said, "Ouch, that looks painful; let's get you cleaned up." The second phrase avoids minimizing and validates their feelings.
>
> 1. *Malicious and intentional gaslighting*- this is more common

and is blatant emotional manipulation. This is where you might hear, "This is your fault; you are so emotionally unstable we can never plan anything." Or "Geez, I was just kidding. Would you calm down?"

Phases:

As I mentioned, the malicious gaslighter will bait you in slowly, creating confusion and leaving you feeling crazy by the end. At the beginning of your relationship, you might make excuses for the abuser's behavior. You want to defend him.

Then, you slowly start to lose your grasp on what is happening. You get confused quickly and find yourself apologizing all the time. You have no idea what you did wrong. You start feeling like you are walking on eggshells. You begin to feel as if something is off.

Finally, you slip into depression. Your self-esteem has been whittled away to nothing. The abuser will constantly remind you of all the self-work you need to do. They will project their own insecurities and shame onto you. They may even call you a narcissist or say you should get evaluated for borderline personality disorder.

You love and trust this person. You believe them and are desperate to salvage the relationship. You start taking online quizzes to see if you are a narcissist or have Borderline Personality Disorder. You are looking for a psychiatrist. You are willing to do anything.

Signs You Are Being Gaslighted

- Isolation
- Increased anxiety
- Feeling like you can't say or do anything right
- Sensing something is wrong but not being able to pinpoint it
- Apologizing often, even when you are unsure what you did
- Feeling insecure

- Feeling like you are walking on eggshells
- Feeling like something is wrong with you

The Light at The End of The Tunnel

You may have taken online quizzes that made you feel better because they showed you were at very low risk of a personality disorder. You were brutally honest with your answers. Maybe you took it a step further and had a professional evaluation, but you were still low risk and were not diagnosed.

Now, you decide to leave the abuser. You put the pieces together and realize the patterns of projection and gaslighting. You block that person and move on. They will lose their mind because now they are left to face their own dark feelings. They will smear your reputation.

Keep going. The truth will set you free. You should be incredibly proud of yourself for breaking free. The abuser's true colors will eventually show so there is no reason to retaliate.

Conclusion

Does any of this sound familiar?

When I finally broke free from my five-year on-and-off relationship with a narcissist, I saw articles that confirmed I had been gaslighted and manipulated in many ways. It validated my decision to terminate the relationship. I was amazed at how many people have been through what I endured.

Had I stayed in that "boat" being drowned by the waves, I eventually would have been catapulted to sea to be eaten by the sharks, both literally and metaphorically.

Recognizing and understanding what gaslighting is, can save your mental well-being. If you experienced it, you might need therapy — not because there is anything wrong with you, but because the abuser likely robbed you of your identity. Gaslighting can actually cause relationship PTSD.

It helped me to start a new hobby, say positive affirmations, and practice being gentle and loving with myself to rebuild my self-esteem and reduce my anxiety. I hope those things will help you as well.

Surround yourself with loving, supportive people. Explain to your friends and family what you went through. Unfortunately, because of the damage the abuser left in their wake, it may take time to repair trust. Set boundaries and never stop believing in yourself. You are stronger than you may realize.

Reference:
Encyclopedia Britannica 2024 https://www.britannica.com/topic/gaslighting
"Falling down is an accident. Staying down is a choice." ~ Author Unknown

The Trail of Breadcrumbs from a Narcissist

Imagine Hansel and Gretel's parents trying to abandon them in the woods, but the kids were wise enough to leave a trail of breadcrumbs to find their way back. Just like Hansel and Gretel, narcissists will do whatever they have to for approval and love.

Today, breadcrumbing refers to someone who gives you enough attention and flirts to keep you on the hook, but they do not provide quality time, deep conversation, or commitment.

The narcissist uses love bombing, which includes compliments, romantic emojis, and flirtatious conversations that lure you in — similar to the evil witch who lured Hansel and Gretel in with sweets. Love bombing is one way to breadcrumb you. They pull you in and get your interest, and then they may disappear because they are not emotionally capable of closeness.

After being with a narcissist, one of the biggest challenges is explaining what happened and making sense of it all.

One moment they were your dream come true, and the next, the devil in disguise.

The narcissist baits you in with tiny sweet suggestive morsels, breadcrumbs, which lead you nowhere. They keep you interested and invested in them while you are an option rather than a priority to them. You have become their supply. You make them feel good, but they drain your energy.

Signs Of Bread Crumbing

- Love bombing.
- They flirt but do not ask you out.
- They "like" and leave comments on your social media, but

they won't return your DM's.
- They will say, "let's meet up," but they do not follow through with a day and time.
- They won't introduce you to friends or family.
- If you stop giving them attention, they love bomb you again.

Stages of The Relationship

The narcissist is passive-aggressive and gaslights you, so you feel confused. They project and then stonewall. Then they leave a trail of breadcrumbs, compliments, and nice gestures to bait you back in. Then, they minimize your feelings and concerns. And, when you finally realize what is happening and leave them, they launch a smear campaign. They never loved you to begin with. The breadcrumbs are poisonous, and feed lies because they rely on your validation and attention.

When a narcissist sees you recognize the manipulation, they devalue you. This is a good sign because it means you are aware and near the end. Hold on tight, though, because they want you to suffer before they discard you and move on to their next victim.

They pull away from you and spend time with other people. My ex-narcissist joined a kickboxing class and would go to dinner or drinks with his classmates after. He started talking specifically about one of the cute girls he had met. He wanted to hurt me, but only to get a reaction.

Tips To Avoid Bread Crumbing

- Be aware of what breadcrumbing is.
- Set firm boundaries.
- Know your self-worth.

Final Thoughts

A relationship should be an equal partnership rather than one person taking and the other giving. Ensure your personal, emotional, physical, and intellectual needs are met. If they are not, it may be time to move on.

Not everyone who breadcrumbs is narcissistic. People with insecure attachments and very emotionally unavailable people may subconsciously do this. It is not as manipulative as gaslighting, but breadcrumbing is a dangerous emotional manipulation that leaves you confused and lonely.

Make sure your partner's words and actions align. If the only time you see this person is to hook up sexually, that is a big red flag. Look for consistency. Stand up for the love, attention, affection, and respect you deserve.

References:

Becky Spelman, a leading Psychologist in the UK, explains Breadcrumbing: https://theprivatetherapyclinic.co.uk/blog/breadcrumbing-how-to-stop-settling-for-maybe/#:~:text=Dealing%20with%20Self%20Esteem%3A%20People,a%20sense%20of%20emotional%20fulfilment.

"Don't get lost in your pain. Know that one day your pain will become your cure." ~ Rumi

Identifying Narcissistic Abuse

Photo by Photo by Sivani Bandaru on Unsplash

Stage 1-Love Bombing

After just a couple of dates, he showers you with compliments, buys you cards and gifts, and creates the illusion he cherishes you. You fall head over heels. You are physically and emotionally drawn to each other. He seemingly does all the right things... until you get comfortable.

"You will go from being the perfect love of their life to nothing you do is ever good enough. You will give everything and they will take it all and give you less in return. You will end up depleted emotionally, mentally, spiritually, and probably financially and then get blamed for it." ~Bree Bonchay

Stage 2-Something Seems Off

You may initially feel like the person you are with is entitled and cannot admit to their mistakes, but the problem runs much deeper than that. It is crucial to recognize the classic red flags and ways a narcissist will manipulate you. Also, identify the way you feel.

You will notice, in time, less physical affection and sexual interest. You will start to feel like you annoy someone who once supposedly adored you.

Clinical Narcissism is a diagnosable mental health condition called narcissistic personality disorder (NPD). Someone with NPD typically lacks empathy and is highly manipulative. They may not be diagnosed because, as we know, "narcissists do no wrong" (I say that sarcastically), but if you recognize these toxic traits — RUN.

"No one can ruin a special occasion like a narcissist who is not the center of attention." ~Author Unknown

Stage 3-Red Flags Surface

1. Gaslighting is a form of manipulation that causes you to question your sanity.
2. Blame-shifting is where the narcissist refuses to take personal responsibility and instead blames you. Sadly, in time, you believe it.
3. Withholding as a form of control. They may withhold money and ask you for permission to do everything. They may withhold sex or conversation.
4. They lack respect for your boundaries. They may invade your privacy by checking your phone or tracking your location.
5. Isolation- friends and family may start to worry because they do not see or talk to you. The narcissist will convince you they are bad influences or say something untrue about you.

The manipulation will increase until you are completely exhausted. Your self-esteem will be depleted, you won't have any friends, and you will start to question why he would love you.

It is the saddest relationship, in my experience, because it started so hopeful and magical. But it was all a lie to bait you in. Narcissists choose a partner that makes them look good. They chose you because you are intelligent, successful, and beautiful.

Yet, you do not relate to any positive qualities you once knew you had because narcissists leave you feeling empty and worthless. They self-sabotage and push those they love away even though they fear abandonment and rejection. It is a self-fulfilling prophecy.

"Narcissists reveal themselves by projecting their bad qualities onto you. They accuse you of the very things they are guilty of. They may even turn everything around and accuse you of being a narcissist. Narcissists cannot handle the reality of who they are, so they project it onto the people around them. They hate that part of themselves, so the best way to get rid of the characteristics they despise is to say it is the other person who is actually engaging in those bad behaviors." ~Maria Consiglio

The Final Discard Stage

Signs You Are Being Psychologically Abused

- mental exhaustion
- low self-esteem
- feeling like you are walking on eggshells
- feeling like you cannot say or do anything right
- physical symptoms such as migraines, lack of sleep, and IBS
- fear of voicing your opinion
- lack of conflict resolution

The manipulation is hard to spot at first, but once the narcissist feels he has worn you down, he may abuse you verbally. He will use words to oppress you:

- *saying you are overreacting*
- *name calling*
- *Sarcasm*
- *Shaming*
- *Blaming*
- *using harsh criticism*

Trauma Bond

"The Brains Betrayal- The hot and cold cycle of attention followed by neglect, or kindness followed by malice, will create a human trauma bond. Your brain will oscillate between pumping out oxytocin (bonding hormone) and cortisol (stress hormone). The intensity and instability of this chemical cocktail breed well the hurricane inside your skill and heart. You feel unsafe. A simmering background of anxiety floods your state, undermining your wellbeing. It becomes difficult to sleep or focus. Brain chemistry plays a massive role here. To stay sane through the process, you need to understand the brain's prime motivation and mechanics. Your brain's main goal is to keep you safe, not happy. Happiness becomes attainable only after your brain is convinced you are safe." ~ Ewa Wonarz

So, you have had enough. Conflicts never get resolved, and the narcissist talks in circles rehashing past mistakes and blaming you. This is called word salad. You decide to leave the relationship.

But you cannot escape the hold a narcissist has on you. He will call and text you, saying everything you want to hear again. He may even cry and apologize. This is the baiting process. He needs to win; he needs to feel good and to do so, he has to get you back.

You cave into his pleas because you *want to believe* he loves you. He promises to do better as a partner.

Until he regains control over you...

Then bam! He bashes you down. This is the process of a trauma bond. You see, he does not want you to have any power. So, he will bait you in and then bash you down. (I say he because that was my experience but women can do this to men as well.) The emotional highs and lows of trauma bonds are devastating.

You may stay in the relationship, or it may be on again and off again for years until you are finally aware of the repeated cycle. It took me five years, to be exact, to learn the pattern. Friends and family all knew to expect another breakup — it was only a matter of time.

Nothing changes with a narcissist. The relationship does not provide the emotional security you need. In fact, it can cause post-traumatic stress syndrome due to ongoing verbal and psychological abuse.

Once you know the baiting and bashing process of trauma bond leaves for good. Block the narcissist on social media and on your phone. Do not try to find out how he is doing through friends. Do not look back. If he gets an inch, he will take a mile. He will email you and may even get a "burner" phone or call you from a no-caller ID number. Do not answer numbers you don't know. If he leaves a voicemail, do not listen. Just delete. He will try his best to bait you back in.

You have to find the strength to stay away from him. It is not easy. You may feel a spectrum of emotions, from betrayal and anger to sorrow. Allow yourself to feel each emotion as it surfaces. Expert Therapists at Sandstone Care* say the trauma bond is equally as challenging to break as quitting opioid addiction.

The narcissist will present themselves as a helpless puppy. You will try your hardest to save/ rescue them. But it is an impossible battle. That "puppy" will continue to run and admire new homes because of their deep childhood wound and insecure attachment style. They have terrible difficulty with compliments, let alone emotional intimacy.

It may help to journal, say positive affirmations, and even join a support group. Therapy or coaching will also help build your self-esteem back up. You lost a large part of your identity in the narcissist through his manipulation. Find a hobby or interest to get involved with and connect with yourself again. Surround yourself with supportive people.

Conclusion

If you are awakening to the possibility that the person you love is a narcissist, it is okay. Awareness is the catalyst for change. Be gentle with yourself. You may or may not be ready to leave the relationship, which is okay.

When you have had enough and see the pattern of trauma bond, you will know. It is heartbreaking. I feel for you. Take your time and grieve. Forgive yourself.

You deserve to be treated with kindness and respect. When the time is right, you will find the perfect mate. Set boundaries and practice self-acceptance.

Reference

*Deborah Quinn and Sarah Fletcher (2024) What is Trauma Bonding? Retrieved from https://www.sandstonecare.com/blog/trauma-bonding/

"You tried so hard to shatter my spirit but a soul full of love can never be broken." ~ *Christy Ann Martine*

Intentional Or Not, Stonewalling is A Toxic Tactic

Stonewalling is a form of emotional abuse where the abuser refuses to communicate. It is a form of gaslighting because it leaves the victim feeling confused, lonely, and frustrated. The abuser refuses to participate in a discussion and acts as if the victim's concern has no value.

Well-known psychologist and relationship expert John Gottman includes stonewalling in what he calls The Four Horseman of The Apocalypse * because it is known to destroy relationships.

Narcissists often use this toxic tactic to regain control of the situation and manipulate their victims. Withholding emotional support creates instability in relationships.

What Stonewalling Looks Like

- Refusal to negotiate or compromise
- Refusal to listen to another person with an open mind
- Refusal to support the other person
- Refusal to accept personal accountability or apologize
- Refusal to communicate
- Silent treatment
- Walking out in the middle of a heated conversation
- Minimizing your significant other's concerns
- Passive-aggressive behavior

There Are Two Types of Stonewalling

1. Unintentional — someone who suffers from PTSD or CPTSD may tend to isolate when confronted with stress. Conflict may send them into shutdown mode, and they likely

want to avoid fighting. This is not the manipulative type of stonewalling but an ineffective coping mechanism to self-soothe. They may not even realize they are doing it.
2. Intentional and manipulative — this tactic controls another person, confuses them, and devalues their concerns.

Reasons For Stonewalling

- Fear their partner will reject them
- Inability to handle the stressful conversation
- Intentional manipulation
- PTSD

Research suggests that 85% of people who use this tactic are men *. It is a form of withholding emotional support. The abuser will often walk out of an argument. Their silence may last days, weeks, or even months. It is a complete refusal to compromise.

"Neglect is abusive. Ignoring a person and not caring about who they are, what they want, and what they need is like telling them they are not important, over and over again. Some toxic people use neglect to make you feel insignificant and unworthy." ~ Maria Consiglio

Are You Stonewalling Without Awareness?

Do you escape or avoid conflict, get defensive, or isolate yourself to avoid difficult conversations or conflict? Do you believe you are always right? If you answered yes, you may be stonewalling your significant other and damaging your relationship.

Why Stonewalling is Damaging

- diminishes all forms of intimacy
- causes frustration
- causes loneliness
- causes resentment
- causes rejection

Rooted in fear and frustration, whether stonewalling is intentional or not, it damages the soul and the relationship.

The Effects of Stonewalling

Stonewalling diminishes all forms of intimacy. Emotional intimacy is cut off the minute the silence and contempt begin. On top of losing the emotional connection, the stress on both people, particularly the man, suppresses sexual urges.

The person being stonewalled sees their partner as unreliable. They start to question themselves and feel like something is wrong with them. It adversely affects their self-worth. This is the perfect scenario for a narcissist who wants to break their partner down so they can control them.

Correcting The Behavior

Learning to self-soothe when you feel emotionally overwhelmed or panicked is the best antidote for stonewalling. Pause and breathe before responding. Announce that you need a time out when necessary but that you will return to the conversation. Minimal conversation and communication are extremely helpful to the victim.

Final Thoughts

Stonewalling causes hypervigilance which is proven to increase heart rate and blood pressure. Take the barriers down that are cutting off oxygen to the relationship.

If you are overwhelmed and need space to process your emotions and think straight, postpone the conversation temporarily and agree to revisit it soon. Be aware of body language and how you are making your partner feel. And, by all means, avoid criticism, name-calling, and eye-rolling — all signs of contempt that will kill a relationship.

References:

Ellie Lisitsa, 2004 The Gottman Institute

The Seven Principles for Making Marriage Work, by John M. Gottman, PH.D, pp32-39

"Feelings are just visitors, let them come and go." ~ Mooji

Understanding Fight or Flight Mode

We all flip out when upset, and here is a scientific reason why...

The fight-or-flight reaction was handed down from our ancestors in the caveman era when they had to choose to fight or flee for their lives. Now, it has evolved into a sequence of hormonal changes and physiological responses to help us cope with stressful situations. Unfortunately, many of us are now hypersensitive, reacting to traffic jams, arguments, and other life stressors as if our lives depended on them.

Anyone who has suffered severe or repeated trauma tends to get trapped living in that survival mode. It is an acute and chronic stress response that makes it difficult to cope with any amount of stress.

Chronic stress triggers an area in the brain called the amygdala, which is the emotional processing center. The amygdala sounds a danger alarm, sending a distress signal to the hypothalamus, the brain's command center. The hypothalamus sends a signal to the nervous system. In the case of fight or flight, it alerts the sympathetic nervous system to give the necessary burst of energy needed to fight or flee for survival.

Physical Signs of Distress, from my personal experience

- rapid heartbeat
- clammy hands
- goosebumps
- nausea
- migraines
- skin rashes

When we experience physical signs of distress, and the sympathetic nervous system is activated, it pumps adrenaline through our body. The body and mind go on high alert. You may experience other physical symptoms, but it is important to be aware.

Meanwhile, the front of the brain contains the cerebral cortex, which regulates reasoning, thinking, and decision-making.

Being in fight-or-flight mode causes irrational and inappropriate reactions that we often regret later. Our thoughts are distorted in this mode, and as a result, we tend to overreact.

Emotions That Often Trigger the Fight-or-Flight Response

- Anger
- Fear
- Aggression
- Betrayal
- Rejection
- Stress

Daniel Goleman put emotional intelligence on the map with his 1995 book *Emotional Intelligence: Why it can matter more than IQ*. People with high levels of emotional intelligence are more self-aware and can see when their emotions are out of balance and quickly regain control.

Preventing Fight-or-Flight Mode

The best way to prevent activating the sympathetic nervous system and going into survival mode, or staying there too long, is to learn what triggers you into a state of hyperarousal. Next, learn how to self-soothe when you become triggered to return to the parasympathetic state where you are calm and rational.

A trigger is anything that causes you to recall a bad memory or experience, which sends a signal to the amygdala that you are in danger.

Triggers can be anything from smells, places, something someone says, or a song.

When the sympathetic nervous system is activated, and we go into fight-or-flight, the goal is to return to the parasympathetic state as quickly as possible. As you can imagine, when the body is running on all cylinders, trying to keep us "alive," it cannot repair tissue or even digest food. It has one goal, and that is to keep us safe. The parasympathetic nervous system is often referred to as the rest and digest state. The body starts to perform much like a Porche running on all cylinders with hardly any oil.

In survival mode, fight-or-flight, the body not only cannot process food and, repair tissue but hormonal production is halted. This is why sex drive is obsolete in high-stress situations.

Tools That I Recommend to Soothe Triggers and Return to the Parasympathetic State

I am supplying some common self-soothing techniques, but it is important to learn what works best for you.

- breath work
- yoga
- exercise
- grounding techniques
- going outside
- listening to calming music

Intentional, deep, slow breathing is one of the best tools for activating the parasympathetic nervous system, which brings us out of fight-or-flight mode and back to a calm, restorative state. Deep breathing literally slows our heart rate, providing calmness; putting us back in a parasympathetic state.

Final Thoughts

When physical signs of stress and anxiety are present, the body sends you a physical message. This message informs you that you are in survival mode and in a sympathetic state. If you were a sports car, it would be equivalent to putting the vehicle into turbocharge mode. It is unrealistic to expect the body to perform at such a high rate for a very long time.

Chronic, long-term stress and anxiety will cause damage to the body and mind. Learn to recognize what triggers you and how to self-soothe to return to a calm state as soon as possible.

"Often, it is the deepest pain that empowers you to grow into your highest self."
~ Karen Salmansohn

The Opposite of a Narcissist: Empaths and Echoists

Understanding Empaths and Echoists

There are two answers to what the opposite of a narcissist is: an empath and an echoist. Narcissists lack empathy and are attracted to empaths because they thrive on their energy, attention, and compliments. Empaths live to please others, which makes them easy prey for manipulation.

The opposite of a narcissist has also been dubbed an echosit. In Greek Mythology, Narcissus fell in love with his own reflection, thus the term narcissist. Echo was a wood nymph deprived of a voice. She fell in love with Narcissus. Psychologist, Craig Malkin, developed the concept of echoism as someone who is voiceless and only exists to echo others.

An echoist has a fear of being the center of attention. They are warm-hearted, giving, and compassionate, which, like empaths, makes them an easy target for a narcissist and vulnerable to abuse.

Empaths struggle to stand up for themselves and, like echoists, lack boundaries. Both are emotional sponges. They give love and sympathy, trying to relieve the pain they know the narcissist is carrying.

Without realizing it, an empath can be emotionally manipulative, much like a narcissist.

Qualities of An Echoist

- avoids the spotlight
- low self-esteem
- loves to "fix" others
- has difficulty asking for help

- lacks boundaries
- timid

Qualities of An Empath

- highly intuitive
- detail-oriented
- absorbs the moods of others
- needs time alone
- is a target for energy vampires
- finds solitude in nature
- has a huge giving heart

You can see where both would be attractive targets for narcissists who need them to look good and mask the shame and fear they carry. Opposites attract, but not always for a good reason.

A narcissist strings their victim along with just enough breadcrumbs to keep them willing to

supply their needs. They play on their victim's willingness to forgive.

An echoist may be more extreme than an empath in that they also have a lot of empathy, but they reject attention and fear praise. Echoists and empaths are often confused with co-dependency. They are good listeners, but unlike co-dependents, they do not try to guide or fix the narcissist.

Echoists typically stem from being raised by a narcissist. This may, in fact, be why they are attracted to the familiarity of a narcissist. Unlike narcissistic personality disorder, echoism is not classified as a mental disorder, yet it is detrimental to their mental health.

Echoists are terrified of confrontation, primarily because they lack their own voice or opinion. They have a strong desire to avoid narcissists and yet are attracted to them. They balance each other because the echoist avoids attention while the narcissist thrives on it. Fear of seeming narcissistic in any way is the defining quality of an echoist. Echoists bury their own needs to gain acceptance.

Final Thoughts

Awareness is the key to change. Follow that awareness with therapy in order to avoid being caught in the narcissist's trap. Empaths and echoists are very creative and should focus on their personal hobbies like painting, poetry, writing, acting, and cooking.

If one or both of your parents were narcissistic, you hate attention, and you often blame yourself when things go wrong, you may be an empath or echoist. Learn your own values and know that your opinions are relevant.

Practice self-acceptance and love, build your self-esteem, and trust your intuition. Narcissists and people with strong narcissistic traits will pounce on any opportunity they see as a supply of energy and deception they need. Remember, with a narcissist; it is not an equal partnership. Protect yourself.

References:

Hope Gillette, October 11, 2022, Medically reviewed by Jennifer Litner, PhD, LMPT, CST The Echo and The Narcissist on Psych Central: https://psychcentral.com/lib/narcissus-and-echo-the-myth-and-tragedy-of-relationships-with-narcissists#recap

Karen Dempsey, an accredited psychotherapist wrote How to Tell if You are an Echosit on The Awareness Center https://theawarenesscentre.com/echoist/

"People who have revived themselves after almost drowning in trauma do not get enough credit. Even though the pain was massive they did not stay stagnant or bitter. They knew the only way out was through the path of healing and they used it to start a new life." ~ Yung Pueblo

Understanding Trauma Bond

Photo by Envato Elements Purchased Image License M5ZFQ6UE2T

Understanding Trauma Bond

A trauma bond is a disturbing connection between the Narcissist and their victim. The Narcissist creates a distinctive attachment by forming a repetitive emotional cycle starting with love-bombing, which baits their victim in. Love-bombing might include compliments, eye contact, romantic gestures, and gifts.

They then build trust through positive reinforcement. When the victim feels comfortable and safe, the Narcissist pulls the rug out from under them and bashes them down. The bash cycle might include stone-walling, gaslighting, name-calling, passive-aggressive behavior, or criticism.

The Narcissist appears to show remorse during the baiting stage, and the victim feels sorry for her partner.

Often, the Narcissist has experienced childhood abuse *. They have a deep fear of abandonment and rejection. The bait-and-bash tactic of trauma bond is similar to what we see in fearful-avoidant and disorganized attachment styles *. A Narcissist creates conflict to ensure control in the relationship.

Why It Happens

Narcissists are attracted to empaths. As empaths, we are naturally sensitive and want to please our mates. They enjoy this because they need their ego to be stroked. This helps them because, deep down, they do not love and accept themselves as a result of their childhood trauma.

You, as a victim, also enjoy the attention and false sense of acceptance that the narcissist provides. In the love bombing and positive reinforcement stages, they make you feel safe and secure. You feel like a power couple.

It doesn't take long for the narcissist to isolate their victim, talk poorly behind their back, and paint a very different picture of you to other people, all the while creating a false sense of security until they are ready to bash you down again.

Recovering

Recovering from the Psychological Effects of trauma bond can take a long time. Working with a mental health professional can help process the trauma and manage the symptoms of PTSD you likely have.

Breaking free from trauma bond is compared to the difficulty of breaking the addiction to opioid drugs because the brain is wired for the cycle of love followed by abuse. It is euphoric at first but then destroys your sense of self.

It takes several break-up make-up sessions with a narcissist, sometimes over the course of years, to realize you are trauma-bonded.

Once you realize what is happening, the real question is, how long will you continue to let the cycle repeat? Take your power back. Leave and rebuild your self-esteem. The narcissist chose you because you are amazing. Never forget that. Do not let their smear campaigns and nasty tactics get in your mind, heart, or soul.

* Jaquelin Johnson (2023) and Lois Zoppi . Trauma Bonding explained. Medical News Today. Retrieved from https://www.medicalnewstoday.com/articles/trauma-bonding#Why-does-it-happen?

*Melissa Porrey, Lpc, Ncc(December 22, 2023), Medically reviewed by Steven Gans, Md How to Recognize a Trauma Bond

https://www.verywellhealth.com/trauma-bonding-5210779

*Lawrence Robinson, JeanneSegal, Ph.D and Jaelline Jaffe, Ph.D Attachment Styles and How they Affect Relationships

https://www.helpguide.org/articles/relationships-communication/attachment-and-adult-relationships.htm#:~:text=Disorganized%2Fdisoriented%20attachment%2C%20also%20referred,or%20closeness%20in%20a%20relationship.

"To heal a wound, you need to stop touching it." ~ The Break-Up Cure

Escaping the Illusion of Love Created by a Narcissist

Recognize the signs of trauma-bond manipulation and psychological abuse.

Dear Narcissistic Abuse Victim,

I am sorry for the pain, frustration, and confusion you must feel. You enter a relationship and make yourself entirely vulnerable for your partner. You feel like they are your soulmate. They make you feel loved and cherished. You share your deepest secrets and all of your insecurities.

And then...BOOM. Around three to six months in, everything changes. Suddenly you feel like you cannot do anything right. The man you loved is now using your insecurities and deepest secrets against you. He doesn't like your friends, so you become isolated and feel like you are constantly walking on eggshells. Sound familiar?

You did nothing differently. You are perplexed as to why the man you love is treating you the

way he is. Yes, you make mistakes, but that is human nature. He makes them too. So, what is really happening?

Trauma Bond 101 *

- A trauma bond is a push-pull cycle that keeps you from returning to a psychologically abusive relationship with a narcissist. Unless you have experienced it, it is difficult to understand why anyone would return to someone who treats them so poorly. But I stayed in that relationship for five years before realizing what was happening.
- The brain tricks you because your man (or, in fairness, woman) will bait you in with kindness, and when you are

comfortable again, he will bash you down. It is a hot and cold cycle. The brain will produce oxytocin (happy hormones) when he is kind and cortisol (stress hormones) when he is cruel. The instability causes a storm within your heart and soul. It leaves you feeling emotionally unsafe and insecure.
- Most days, you do not know if you are coming or going. You desperately want the relationship to work, and yet you question why. You start feeling crazy because the man you love is so manipulative. *And he is darn good at it.*
- You try to fix all the problems and study how to be a better partner because he has convinced you that you are the one doing everything wrong or overreacting.
- You take online personality tests because the man you love repeatedly tells you that you have borderline personality disorder or narcissism, even though he is far from qualified to diagnose you.
- Until you break free from the trauma bond and finally escape the *illusion* of love, you won't realize that he was projecting; he was the narcissist.
- A narcissist will feed off your misery because they are energy vampires. They suck the life out of your soul. They feel better when they make people feel bad, especially you. It makes them feel like they have power and influence, but again it is all an illusion. Likely, they also speak badly about their past relationships, which is a red flag.

Psychological Abuse

Their manipulation tactics are psychologically abusive. They take power over your emotions and play you like a marionette. They provoke anger to get a reaction and then blame you and call you abusive. This tactic is reactive abuse, and you are not to feel blamed.

"Reactive abuse: when a victim is abused, antagonized, and gaslighted and finally stands up for themselves. This may be angry words, acts of defiance, or even violence. The retaliation to the abuser. THEN the oppressor calls the victim the abusive one." ~ Author Unknown

In my experience, most narcissists have experienced childhood trauma or neglect. They are terrified of abandonment and lack self-love and acceptance. Narcissism is a form of self-sabotage. On a subconscious level, they are convinced they do not deserve you, which is why they have jealous control issues.

They will tell you everything you want to hear, buy you cards, and court you until you call them out on any minor thing. Then they will punish you. That is where their true colors show. You know someone has class and truly loves you if they leave the relationship respectfully.

A narcissist will use smear campaigns when you leave them. Their anger will rage when you finally tire of their manipulation. Rise above. Please do not listen to the toxic poison they try to feed your mind. Deep down, you know your self-worth. That is why they chose you to begin with. Narcissists do not pick ugly, worthless people — they go for the prize so they will look better.

They do not love themselves. It is not your fault nor your job to make them feel loved. Forgive yourself. You cannot fill that void in their life. What you can do is reinvent yourself and continue to love yourself.

Signs of Emotional Abuse

- Isolating
- Hyper criticism
- Refusing to communicate/ stonewalling
- Domination
- Using statements such as, "If you_____, I will_____" or "If you don't _____ I will_____"

- Guilt trips, placing blame on you, and lack of personal responsibility
- Talking in circles without resolving conflict, dredging up past mistakes
- Destroying your possessions or threatening you
- Using money to control you

If he says any of these things, you are likely being gaslighted:

You are so sensitive
Stop acting crazy
You are so paranoid
I was only kidding
It was no big deal
You are overreacting
Oh, there you go again
Nobody believes you, and nobody cares
We talked about this, remember?
Can't you take a joke?
Stop taking everything so seriously

If these things sound familiar, I want you to surround yourself with supportive people who

allow your Light to shine. Start preparing quietly to leave the relationship. Seek counseling if you are experiencing depression or want to see if his behavior will change. It was my experience that couples therapy did not work. My narcissistic ex could not take any criticism and would not take personal responsibility. Each time I tried to leave; he lashed out worse. Have a plan in place, and if you feel you are ever in harm, please go to the police and court for a protection order. Please do not stay in the relationship out of fear.

If you are having recurring headaches, loss of appetite, hair loss, trouble sleeping, memory loss, or chronic pain. These are physical signs of post-traumatic stress syndrome. Please seek help. You have experienced psychological abuse, and your body and soul are begging for help.

"You cannot heal a person who keeps using their pain as an excuse to hurt you. READ THAT AGAIN." ~ Author Unknown

Conclusion

Each relationship teaches us a lesson, some more than others. After recovering from the emotional and psychological abuse, realize what you have learned so you do not fall for another abusive person. Thank the friends and family that pointed out the abusive behavior they witnessed. It can be challenging to see the abuse while we are in turmoil.

Breaking trauma bonds has been compared to being as challenging as giving up opioid drugs. I have not done drugs, but leaving a narcissist was one of the hardest things I have done.

No contact was the only way I could finally break free after an on-again, off-again relationship for five years. He has tried to email me, WhatsApp me, and reach out to my friends and family. He has written false articles about me and maintains an intense smear campaign. I fell many times when he came back and sincerely apologized. But I learned faster each time that he wanted to hurt me. Each time I returned; he used it against me. He can no longer hurt me because my level of awareness is at an all-time high.

The best part of the smear campaigns and his mean behavior is that letting go is much easier. It makes it easy to forget the good times and to see the monster he really is.

I was in mastermind training with our relationship, and now I am a ninja. I can recognize manipulation and psychological abuse from a mile away. I will not let anyone control me again. I hope you find the strength to leave if you are in an abusive relationship. You are worthy of love, respect, and appreciation.

Reference: Written by the Team at Better Help and Medically reviewed by Julie Dodson, MA (May 2024)
    https://www.betterhelp.com/advice/trauma/what-abusers-hope-we-never-learn-about-traumatic-bonding/?

"Trauma bonding makes you psychologically addicted to abuse. This explains why going no contact feels like coming off a drug." ~ Author Unknown

The Narcissistic Epidemic and How to Battle It

Why So Many People Are Talking About Narcissism

Narcissism is a big buzzword these days. There are hundreds if not thousands of questions about it on Quora and many articles on multiple platforms, and the reason is Narcissists manipulate and devastate their victims. They isolate them, turn their world upside down, and then discard them, usually leaving them alone to search for answers about what just happened to them.

The victim's self-esteem is at rock bottom, and they are ashamed to admit what has happened. They feel like they are the bad person. Reading that other people have experienced narcissistic abuse offers a small amount of comfort. It acknowledges that the victim is not crazy nor alone in their suffering.

The victim experiences so many layers of frustration because they still thought they loved the narcissist. They are in disbelief that the narcissist could betray them on this level. They also feel betrayed by friends who are now the narcissists flying monkeys also saying and doing hurtful things during this smear campaign. Their reputation is tarnished, and as if their low self-esteem is not bad enough now, they are left without a job and broke, and sadly, many become homeless. This doesn't need to happen when you are empowered and have tools to build your self-esteem.

They now have such a limited network of support that they depend on fellow narcissistic abuse survivors.

Was Your Ex-Diagnosed Narcissistic?

Some people get caught up in the label of a diagnosis. If it looks like a skunk, acts like a skunk, and smells like a skunk, it's probably a skunk, and we do not need to get caught up in a label. Someone cruel and manipulative who comes across as charismatic in crowds but abusive behind closed doors is dangerous to the victim's soul regardless of a label.

Final Thoughts

We are hearing more about narcissism now because it is more common and often referred to as an epidemic *. I believe there are far more narcissists roaming around than are diagnosed. A true narcissist will deny they have a problem. In fact, they will project their problems onto you. We live in an age of vanity. Selfies are encouraged. But narcissism is more than vanity; it is evil.

The good news is, on the flip side of narcissism, we are also in the age of a great spiritual awakening. Those who choose can walk a path toward enlightenment. They can skip the selfies and vanity. They can decide to peel away the layers of the subconscious, and to do the shadow work * and to dive deep into the heart of who they are meant to be. Once that work is done, a narcissist can no longer hurt this person as they are protected by the divine.

Be thankful if you have not suffered narcissistic abuse. If you know someone who has, please be empathetic. It is extremely traumatic. It takes a long time to recover.

* Twenge JM, Campbell WK. The narcissism epidemic: Living in the age of entitlement Free Press 2009 https://books.google.com/books?hl=en&lr=&id=m3YndShMSUUC&oi=fnd&pg=PA1&ots=gRsS41f4YO&sig=JgRVI-IEVUjVXkJJbPb8EVxMIPI#v=onepage&q&f=false

* Elizabeth Perry, ACC, The Benefits of Shadow Work and How to Use It in Your Journey. Better Up, 2022 https://www.betterup.com/blog/shadow-work

"We subconsciously seek situations to act out old emotional wounds until we are able to heal them." ~ Dr. Nicole LePela

The Cycle of The Narcissist Breaking No Contact

Photo by Envato Elements Purchased Image License MJRKDBTP6F

Why They Won't Let Go

It has been my personal experience that a narcissist will refuse to let go after a breakup. Even when you have no contact, they will find a way to continue to harass you. They cannot stand the fact that you have moved on.

Narcissists and people with strong narcissistic tendencies have low self-esteem and a massive fear of abandonment. Narcissists refuse to admit it is over and hoover * to suck you back in.

Reasons They Break No Contact

- Validation
- He misses you
- He wants to hook up
- He feels Guilty
- He wants the control back (this is a big one)

In my experience, my ex did not break the "no contact" because of curiosity or the need for closure. It was simply selfish. Even though my ex knows I am in a healthy relationship, he continues to email me. The emails go into my junk folder, but I check that account periodically for work emails. I have now gotten to the point where I don't even open them.

Narcissists use a bait-and-bash technique to keep you trauma bonded to them. Sometimes, my ex would say the most hurtful things; other times, he was kind and supportive. Do not fall for their kindness — it is a trap.

The Cycle of A Narc Breaking No-Contact

First, they will blame you and then tell you how much they love you. Quickly following the love-bombing, they will cuss you out, call you names, and bash you down. Then, they will send you a YouTube video of a song. Do not click the link because it will pull on your heartstrings. When you do not respond, he lacks the attention he craves and feels rejected. His anger sets in. Then he will launch a smear campaign and tell your family things they were never intended to know. Those are intimate details you only share with the "person you love."

Do not panic when he reveals your secrets. People will see your true colors as well as his destructive tendencies. He wants to upset you so that you will reach out and communicate with him.

Final Thoughts

Block him on social media and your phone. Send emails to junk. You will likely read them until you become familiar with this toxic cycle. Eventually, you will learn not to open them. If you struggle with staying away from him, try writing down all the times he manipulated and verbally abused you. Write down the cycles you have become familiar with. This will remind you of how painful leaving was and help prevent you from staying trauma-bonded.

Get involved in new hobbies and activities. Build your confidence by saying positive affirmations. You deserve a partner who respects you and can control their emotions.

*Darlene Lancer,JD, LMFD Why Narcissists and Abusers Won't Let Go and What You Can Do Psychology Today, 2021

https://www.psychologytoday.com/us/blog/toxic-relationships/202103/why-narcissists-and-abusers-wont-let-go-and-what-you-can-do

*Clinically approved by Silvana Mici, Coach, Written by Sylvia Smith, Author Why Do Men Come Back After No Contact: 23 Strong Reasons Marriage.com, 2024

https://www.marriage.com/advice/relationship/why-men-come-back-after-no-contact/

*The Joint Commissions

The California Department of Health Care Services

The National Association of Addiction Treatment Providers: Trauma Bonding: What is It and Why Do We Do It? A Mission For Micheal, 2024

https://amfmtreatment.com/trauma-bonding-what-is-it-and-why-do-we-do-it/

"When you shut down emotion, you are also affecting your immune system, your nervous system. So the repression of emotion, which is a survival strategy, then becomes a source of physiological illness later on." Gabor Mate

Breaking Free from the Agony of Covert Psychological Abuse

The effects of covert psychological abuse from an intimate partner are profound and long-lasting. The first thing on the internet that pops up when researching covert psychological abuse is the Domestic Violence Help Hotline which proves how serious this is. Covert abuse is quiet, stealthy, and often hard to pinpoint, whereas overt abuse is loud and obvious.

The abuser will use your insecurities and vulnerabilities to distort your reality, confuse you, and make you feel crazy.

If you start questioning yourself and researching these questions, you are likely in a covert abusive relationship.

- Is he really abusing me, or am I overreacting?
- Am I the toxic one?
- Should I apologize and fix the relationship?
- Should I stay in the relationship each time he promises how sorry he is?

Do you feel like you have lost yourself? Trust your intuition or gut feeling if you are researching to determine why you are so strung out, sad, and even depressed. You are very likely being covertly abused.

Signs of Covert Psychological Abuse That I Experienced

1. sleep deprivation
2. feeling like you cannot say or do anything right
3. feeling like you are walking on eggshells
4. raised stress and anxiety levels
5. feeling isolated and depressed

Does your partner tell you that you are overreacting or too sensitive? Do they act as if *they* are the victim? They may even accuse you of being a narcissist; mine sure did.

Tactics Covert Psychological Abusers Use

- lying
- minimizing your thoughts and feelings
- sarcasm while making fun of you
- gaslighting
- passive aggressive behavior
- projection
- blame-shifting
- shrugs shoulders when you question them
- rehashes old arguments and talks in circles
- storms out of disagreements

The abuser will love-bomb you initially, and watching the relationship deteriorate slowly is devastating. You see the decline, but you can't understand why.

How the Relationship Plays Out

Looking back, it is as if you lived in a real-life horror story. The abuser will play the victim and blame you, but you can now see the manipulation tactics. When you try to leave, they will look for sympathy from you and bait you back in. Block them and never look back, and you will temporarily block and play mind games occasionally until the patterns of abuse and manipulation become crystal clear.

They will look to friends and family for sympathy and validation when they cannot get to you and regain your attention.

This off-and-on cycle of your relationship may go on for months or even years before you see the pattern clearly and are strong enough to leave forever. You may block and then unblock because you feel bad for them or may even be convinced it was your fault.

Breaking Free

As I have explained, covert abuse includes gaslighting, stonewalling, projection, and other manipulative tactics to brainwash you into a state of utter confusion. Part of you believes you are being mistreated or abused, but the other part is in disbelief. Breaking free can be a long, tumultuous, and agonizing process.

Your abuser may ramp up in anger when they see signs of you disengaging. They may punch holes in the wall or even do property damage. Mine did both. He actually cut the Christmas tree lights so that I couldn't light the tree after we spent hours decorating outside.

They may keep you up all night talking or having sex. This is simply another manipulative tactic to cause you to have brain fog and be irritable.

The truth is no matter how badly you want to save this relationship, it is not possible. It is not only toxic but dangerous.

Healing to Move Forward and Onward

Healing and recovering from covert psychological abuse requires you to spend time alone. Solitude might feel peaceful to you. You have likely lost some of your identity through abusive brainwashing. Take your time and rebuild your self-esteem. The abuser probably made you question your intuition, so now is the time to strengthen that self-trust.

1. Sit with your emotions as they surface — journal to better understand. Identify what triggers you and how to calm yourself down. Learn how your body physically responds to those emotions that trigger you. They are sending you a message. For example, if your heart starts pounding and your palms are sweating, your body signals danger. With awareness, you are better suited to cope with those stressors.
2. Set boundaries. Setting boundaries and enforcing them

protect your emotions. If someone does not respect those boundaries, they do not respect you. Run away fast.
3. Come out of isolation and surround yourself with people who believe in and support you.
4. Once you are confident and ready to leave your abusive partner, be prepared because they will launch a smear campaign. They will reveal and expose all of your insecurities. Although it is painful that any monster could do this, it will confirm you made the right decision to end the relationship.

Your abusive partner had very low self-esteem. They need this outside validation to survive. Although your self-esteem is likely at an all-time low when you leave the relationship, please know your abuser chose you because of your beauty, talents, and character.

Final Thoughts

Covert psychological abuse cannot be seen externally like overt and physical abuse, but it dims the light in our souls. I consider it the death of a million paper cuts. This invisible abuse creates deep emotional wounds that are as serious and damaging as physical abuse.

If you are in danger, please call the Domestic Help Hotline at 800–799–7233 or text START to 88788. Psychological abuse can quickly escalate into physical abuse.

References:
Kathie Mathis, Psy.D, NCP, DAPA Covert and Overt Narcissist; California Cognitive, 2022 https://theccbi.com/covert-and-overt-narcissist/
Heather Jones What are the Signs of Love Bombing? ; Very Well Health, 2023 https://www.verywellhealth.com/what-is-love-bombing-5224664
"Never wish them pain. That's not who you are. If they caused you pain, they must have pain inside. Wish them healing. That is what they need." ~ Najwa Zebian

Only Narcissists Defend Narcissists- Flying Monkeys

Photo by Envato Elements Purchased Image License VU6YLJW57M

Have you ever dated a narcissist? If so, you know the damaging effects. I literally feel like I am living in a Lifetime Original Horror Movie. I have spent more time with my therapist lately than I care to admit. She is a lovely woman, but it is summer, and I would rather be barefoot outside doing something far more relaxing than working through painful memories of my narcissistic ex.

The odd thing is once you date one narc, you tend to be a magnet to more; at least, I did. The good news is you also learn to recognize the signs much faster. I had to dive deep into my patterns and am still healing. I am an empath, and narcissists prey on empaths. Each relationship has torn me open wider, though, and allowed for even more clarity and healing.

I feel like I am an expert on narcissism after this third one.

Whoa, he had me convinced he wasn't even a narcissist; he was so good until the very end. But, when he sent the flying monkeys out, that was his tell. Fortunately, by the time I reached that relationship, I had established firm boundaries and would not tolerate abuse.

What are Flying Monkeys

Remember the scary flying monkeys in The Wizard of Oz that were released to spy and gather information and then return it to the wicked witch? That is essentially what flying monkeys are *. They are friends and family of the narcissist that collect information and spread all your deepest darkest secrets to tarnish your reputation and try to make the narcissist appear better.

Only Narcissists Defend Narcissists*

True colors always shine through. In each breakup, you will have friends who will choose sides. Some will do it with integrity and honesty. Others will be backstabbing. It is up to you to trust your intuition and your gut feeling's, to protect your emotional integrity.

If someone chooses to take the narcissist's side, especially when abuse is involved, they show you that they identify with that person's character. Narcissists are like wolves—they hunt in packs. Chances are, these people have also committed verbal or physical abuse to someone in their lives or may have been abused. These are lying, conniving people.

In my case, my ex-best friend reached out after the physical abuse and offered to be my court advocate. She had prior court experience, but my instinct told me she was up to no good. She then reached out, inviting me to wine tastings, hoping I would divulge court information she could then pass along to my abusive ex. Fortunately, I was wise enough to graciously pass and eventually stop communicating with her.

Ultimately, my intuition was spot on. My ex-best friend and boyfriend conspired against me and started a cyber attack on my writing platforms. They did not want me to be happy and successful because they were miserable. Always remember, misery loves company.

It empowers these so-called friends, *flying monkeys*, to help the narcissist drag you down and tell people every dirty little secret about you. It makes them feel good. It makes them feel powerful. They will even call and act like they are on your side. Do not fall for it. They are only trying to gather information to use against you and give to the narcissist. They will reach out to everyone you know.

Final Thoughts

There is a special place in hell for these people. So, I will hold my head high and continue with my life. If you have been affected by a narcissist or their flying monkeys, I suggest you do the same. They feed on any energy they receive. It is best to let them enjoy their own misery on their own. Sadly, these are sick individuals who suffered in their childhood.

It is very hurtful to not only lose the person you thought you loved and his family but also to lose friends in the process. To see how backstabbing and hurtful people can be is a terrible thing. I didn't ask to be abused. The fact that anyone would or could justify this narcissist's behavior sickens me.

Stay classy and rise above. They can only hurt you emotionally if you let them. ❤

Susan Krauss Whitbourne, PhD, ABPP Do Narcissists of a Feather Flock Together?; Psychology Today, 2016 *https://www.psychologytoday.com/us/blog/fulfillment-any-age/201605/do-narcissists-feather-flock-together#:~:text=In%20interpreting%20the%20f

Claire Jack, PhD Are You a Narcissist's Flying Monkey?; Psychology Today, 2020 *https://www.psychologytoday.com/us/blog/women-autism-spectrum-disorder/202010/are-you-narcissist-s-flying-monkey

"Do not look for healing at the feet of those who broke you." ~Author Unknown

The Damaging Effects of Psychological Narcissistic Abuse

If you suspect you have dated a narcissist, you have been abused. Narcissists use a form of abuse called psychological abuse *. It is often verbal but sometimes covert or hidden and hard to detect. It will leave you questioning your sanity. Having survived physical and psychological abuse, I would argue that the latter causes more long-term damage and suffering. Both are horrible, and no one should have to endure abuse of any kind.

Types Of Psychological Abuse *

- Gaslighting
- Manipulation
- Name-Calling
- Belittling
- Stonewalling
- Projection

Gaslighting, manipulation, and stonewalling are a few that are more covert. A narcissist, or someone with strong narcissistic tendencies, may shut down in public, stonewalling you, and then name-call and ridicule you at home.

How To Cope with Psychological Abuse

Psychological abuse is damaging to the soul. It is often a very lonely feeling. No one can see your wounds as they can with physical abuse, yet you are dreadfully hurt. It leaves you questioning everything. The abuser turns you into someone you aren't, and you no longer recognize yourself, just like the photo of the orange with the tomato inside. They played you like a puppet.

It is essential that you recognize what is happening and leave the abuser. Surround yourself as best you can with supportive people. This may be hard if the narcissist haslaunched a smear campaign * against you. You can count on finding a therapist or minister if you do not have friends or family.

Work on rebuilding your self-esteem. Re-learn who you are separately from who you were with your significant other. Try new hobbies and get to know yourself again. Journaling and saying positive affirmations are helpful.

Positive Affirmations
I am healing each day
I am worthy of love
I am filled with love and abundance

Final Thoughts

Spend time outdoors. Walking in nature can be very healing. Spending time alone allows you to reconnect with yourself. You can stop the external chatter that makes you question everything. You will want to apologize even when you haven't done anything wrong, which is exhausting, so time alone is a respite for the soul.

Parks are a fun option to lift your spirit and have fun with your furry friend. There are many local dog parks, of course too.

If you feel unsafe, carry your phone, and you can purchase mace online. It may take a while before you trust others again. Learn to trust yourself. Listen to your intuition.

Written by Nakpangi Thomas, PhD, LPC, TITC-CT and Medically Reviewed by Dena Westphalen, Pharm.D Narcissistic Abuse: Signs, Effects, & Treatments Choosing Therapy, 2024 *https://www.choosingtherapy.com/narcissistic-abuse/#:~:text=They%20may%20make%20you%20feel,%2C%20spiritual%2C%20or%20sexual%20abuse.

Written by Sajana Gupta Medically Reviewed by Yolana Renteria, LPC What is Psychological Abuse? Very Well Mind, 2022 *https://www.verywellmind.com/psychological-abuse-types-impact-and-coping-strategies-5323701

Written by Kaytee Gillis, LCSW-BACS Medically Reviewed by Rajy Abulhosn, MD Narcissistic Smear Campaign: What is it, Tactics, & How to Deal With it Choosing Therapy, 2023 *https://www.choosingtherapy.com/narcissist-smear-campaign/

"There are wounds that never show on the body that are deeper and more hurtful than anything that bleeds." ~ Author Unknown

Communication With a Narcissist Is Like Opening Pandora's Box

Is It Possible to Escape a Narcissist?

Leaving a relationship with a narcissist is monumentally difficult, mainly because of the trauma bond. The only way to succeed is to have strict no contact. If children are involved, you may have to use the Gray Rock approach to deflect the abusive behavior. The narcissist will try to bait you back in either with love bombing and compliments or with a full-on smear attack. In my situation, he would send sweet emails or love songs tugging at my heartstrings. When I opened the emails, it was like opening Pandora's Box.

Pandora's Box

To understand my analogy, let's look at Greek Mythology. Hesiod related the curiosity that led her to open a container her husband had, which released a curse *. One must exhibit self-restraint to refuse to open the email from the narcissist when you have them blocked on your phone and social media. It is all deceit. They want you to fall for the trickery of opening it to bait you in and make you feel guilty for not having contact. It is terribly tempting because you were in love and wanted your relationship to succeed until you spotted signs of gaslighting, stonewalling, and manipulation.

The narcissist has low self-esteem and is deeply afraid of being abandoned. I fell for the emails for a long time, but suddenly I realized it was opening Pandora's Box, and the nightmare would continue. I am no longer tempted. I no longer care what he wants to communicate about.

He claims I am a narcissist— *projection*. He claims I never loved him—*also projection*. He never loved himself, nor did he accept my love.

I have had enough of the trauma bond and abuse. I will never open Pandora's Box again. Pandora's Box represents several evils, including remorse, envy, ignorance, inconsistency, and poverty, among other evils. A narcissist displays and delivers all of these things. It leaves your heart poverty-stricken and ripped open. You feel ignorant for allowing the pattern to repeat. I am finally remorseful and ashamed that I ever loved that person.

Final Thoughts

Although Hesiod was a woman who opened Pandora's Box and released evil into the world, someone with a Narcissist is lured into deception—man or woman. The narcissist is the evil one. Just avoid falling for it at the cost of your sanity. Breaking a trauma bond has been equated with being as difficult as breaking an opioid addiction. Be strong, stay strong, and do not fall for the evil tactics and manipulation the narcissist will continue. Move on and live the life you are worthy of. Do not worry about the effect of their mudslinging and smear campaign. You know the truth, and other people will see it too.

Ingrid Clayton, PhD What is Trauma-Bonding? Psychology Today, 2021 https://www.psychologytoday.com/us/blog/emotional-sobriety/202109/what-is-trauma-bonding

My Wellbeing Community What is The Gret Rock Method https://mywellbeing.com/for-therapists/grey-rock-technique

Wikipedia, Pandora's Box https://en.wikipedia.org/wiki/Pandora%27s_box

"When you can tell your story and it doesn't make you cry, that is when you know you are healed." ~ Author Unknown

The Cycle with a Narcissist

Five Common Phrases a Narcissist Uses

I heard these phrases often from my last boyfriend. Although he was not clinically diagnosed as a narcissist, it was abundantly clear by his love of himself, disregard for others, lack of empathy, covert tendencies, and projection/victim mentality.

1. *"What about your problems?" Deflection 101.*
2. *"I'm sorry; what more could you possibly want from me?" Victim mentality, passive-aggressive.*
3. *"You caused this to happen." Projection*
4. *"Why do you always bring up the past?" Lack of personal accountability.*
5. *"You didn't let me finish what I was saying." Changing the story to make himself look better.*

Emotional Intelligence and Narcissists

Narcissists are emotionally stunted. They were either physically or emotionally neglected or abused as children *. In the case of my last boyfriend, his parents both worked and were alcoholics, so he was neglected and possibly abused as well. He grew up in a bar—not an ideal setting for a young boy, and it is no shock that he grew up to be an abusive alcoholic with anger problems.

Narcissists have deep fears and insecurities that they project onto other people. Less than .5% are actually diagnosed with Narcissistic personality disorder.

The Cycle with a Narcissist

- Love Bombing
- Bashing you down/ abuse
- Bait You Back

Trauma Bond is the cycle of positive reinforcement followed by abuse, regret, and maybe even apologies, followed by more love and then more hatred and abuse.

They will play the victim and tell everyone how horribly you treat them and how badly their exes treated them. They will make sure everyone knows how much they work on themselves and how much therapy they get. They will launch a full smear campaign and send their flying monkeys after you.

What the narcissist will *not* mention is how much he projects, abuses you, gaslights... They won't tell what they did to you, only what you did out of a reaction to their abuse of you.

Final Thoughts

The only way to break the abusive cycle with a narcissist is to have no contact and never look back. No matter how much you might miss this person, they will never change. The cycle will repeat, and your soul will continue to take a beating. Your self-esteem will get crushed. I went one step further and filed for a permanent court order of protection. If you feel you are in physical harm, I suggest that as well.

References/Educational Resource

*NICBM (2024) National Institute for the Clinical Application of Behavioral Medicine. Treating Narcissism: How to Dissolve Narcissistic Defenses and Foster Client Vulnerability. Retrieved from https://www.nicabm.com/program

Deborah Quinn Sandstone Care, 2024 https://www.sandstonecare.com/

"You cannot go through life allowing pain to dictate how you behave." ~ *Adam Braverman*

Recognizing An Emotionally Safe Relationship

Photo by Envato Elements Purchased Image License SLW89G3UQJ

What an Emotionally Safe Relationship Looks and Feels Like, from my personal perspective and experience

You may be too afraid to trust if you have ever experienced a toxic relationship. However, an emotionally safe relationship will give you the stability and safety you need to heal.

An emotionally Safe Person

- Encourages you to express your feelings.
- They do not seek external validation because they are confident in themself.
- They are authentic and able to be vulnerable.
- They can resolve conflict and grow from constructive criticism.
- They allow you to feel seen, heard and understood.
- They avoid hurtful behaviors like contempt, name-calling,

and stonewalling.

An emotionally safe person will not be controlling or jealous. They will be supportive and interested in your life. An emotionally safe person allows you to feel accepted, understood and appreciated. It is the foundation for a stable, healthy, and happy relationship.

Communication and trust are essential in an emotionally safe relationship. Emotional security evolves from childhood. You may have anxious or avoidant attachment if you have experienced childhood trauma or neglect. An insecure attachment style may cause you to be needy, clingy, self-reliant, or act out. But, with awareness, you can grow more confident, build your emotional intelligence and become secure.

Emotionally Unavailable People

Emotionally unavailable people are hard to read. They mask their flaws and insecurities. They will not communicate consistently. You may have to draw information out of them. They may avoid deep conversations that involve taking personal accountability. They may get overwhelmed by emotional intimacy. They have a Jekyll and Hyde personality that runs hot or cold, all or nothing.

Signs You Are Dating Someone Emotionally Unavailable

- They dismiss your feelings
- You feel like you are walking on eggshells
- They are on one minute and off another
- They do not want to announce any commitment
- They cannot take criticism or admit fault
- They constantly search for and need external validation
- You are not a priority to them

You are Dating Someone Who Lacks Emotional Safety; Now What?

1. Practice active listening.
2. Agree to transparency to build trust.
3. Stop judging each other.
4. Show respect to your partner and treat them the way you want to be treated.
5. Set and respect personal boundaries.
6. Commit to loving, supporting, and appreciating each other.
7. Set and enforce boundaries.

Final Thoughts

Emotional intelligence is essential in relationships because it helps communication, empathy, and the ability to resolve conflict productively. The good news is you can build your emotional intelligence at any age.

Being in an emotionally safe relationship builds security and stability, allowing both people to grow into their best selves. It will make both partners feel accepted and forgiven when they make mistakes. An emotionally safe relationship creates confidence in both partners and fosters a healthy and happy lifestyle.

"Feeling safe in someone's energy is a different type of intimacy. That feeling of peace is really underrated." ~ Vanessa Klas

Learning to Trust

So Many of Us Are Hesitant to Trust

We live in a very distrusting, emotionally guarded society. Many of us have been betrayed by someone we loved. Some of us had adverse childhood experiences that made us skeptical and fearful.

Trust is a critical component of intimate relationships. Cheating is not the only form of betrayal. Breaking promises, missing bids for attention, lying, and manipulation can all cause us to lose trust. Trusting takes faith and patience and requires vulnerability.

"Vulnerability is the birthplace of love, belonging, joy, courage, empathy, and creativity. It is the source of hope empathy, accountability, and authenticity." ~Brene Brown

Signs of Trust in a Relationship

- Commitment to the relationship
- Feeling emotionally safe
- A partner who listens and cares when you share feelings, needs, and concerns
- Complete transparency
- Acceptance and forgiveness
- Loyalty
- Respect for each other (speaking kindly to them, but also about them)
- Helping each other through difficult times
- A sense of stability
- Respecting each other's boundaries
- Comfort
- Appreciation

Open communication is one of the most significant components of building or rebuilding trust. If your partner has breached your trust and you want to repair the relationship, pay attention to their sincerity when you talk. Each partner should avoid eye rolling and snarky tones of voice. Both people must voice their needs, concerns, frustrations, and appreciation for each other.

Accepting and forgiving each other is the best way to continue a healthy relationship. If your partner betrays you, you may blame yourself and must practice self-acceptance and forgiveness.

Steps For Learning to Trust Again

1. Get rooted in your community. Get to know people.

Follow a set daily routine. By doing so, you become familiar with seeing the same people, and that repetition builds trust.

1. Reveal yourself to people, slowly building vulnerability.

Build trust in yourself by listening to your gut instinct and creating a meaningful life.

1. Set and enforce boundaries to protect your emotional well-being.
2. Grow your self-awareness. Recognize emotional and psychological abuse and manipulation.
3. Align yourself with trustworthy people. This will restore your faith that you are worthy of trust.

Repair or Leave?

If you were lied to or cheated on by your significant other, you would need to decide whether you want to try to repair the relationship and restore trust or go your separate ways.

If you choose to stay together, you must understand why it happened to prevent it from recurring. Details are more harmful than helpful. Avoid rehashing the event repeatedly. If you have decided to stay together, both people must be fully committed to each other and the relationship and leave the past in the past.

It may take time to trust your partner again, but it is possible. Having your partner be consistent and ensuring their words and actions align will help.

If you can never trust your partner again, be honest and forthright so you can move forward in life.

When both people are fully committed, your relationship might become more vital than ever. If you were the one who broke the trust, take personal responsibility and show, as well as tell, your partner how sincerely sorry you are. The truth will set you free. If your partner decides not to remain with you, that is the consequence of your actions that you have to contend with.

Be completely honest and open with your partner moving forward. Hiding phones or computers will cause doubt and resentment.

Red Flags of Possible Betrayal

- You jump at the ding of a text in fear your partner is cheating.
- If your partner works late, it worries you sick.
- You are constantly looking for clues.
- Sudden behavior change.

There is no guarantee we won't get hurt. Love is choosing to share your heart with your partner. When your partner is trustworthy, it allows for fantastic peace, freedom, and security.

Final Thoughts

To trust others, we must first learn to trust ourselves. If you have experienced trauma, abuse, neglect, or betrayal, you may want to write off future relationships for fear of being hurt again. Relationships are essential for personal growth.

A life without meaningful relationships lacks luster. Give people a chance, set and enforce boundaries, and trust your gut instinct. If something feels off, it likely is. When someone disrespects your boundaries and needs, they probably do not respect you as a person.

Therapy individually as well as couples therapy could be very helpful for restoring trust.

I have been cheated on, and it was brutal. I felt rejected and as if I wasn't good enough. It took a long time to rebuild my self-esteem. I am finally in a healthy relationship, and I can assure you there is no better feeling. When I was cheated on, my mom said, "Lib, someone who truly loves and respects you would never do anything that could risk losing you." I think that was sage advice.

"As you heal your attractions change too. Toxicity stops looking like excitement, and peace stops looking like boredom." ~ Author Unknown

How Can I Ever Trust Again?

EEnvato Elements Purchased Image License REXHKGVCQY

Trust is a virtue that so many people are afraid to believe in. Most of us walk around second-guessing intentions, even more so when they are kind and friendly. For many, this lack of trust begins with insecure childhood attachments and trauma. For others, it is repeated betrayal throughout life. The big question is, how do we restore trust?

Restoring Trust Starts Within

Ultimately, the only person I must trust is myself. I know this may seem far out to some of you. Others are likely rolling their eyes, either thinking I am some crazy hippy or a narcissist, and I am neither. Fortunately, after a horrible relationship where I was betrayed by a man I thought I loved and wanted to spend my life with, I had a fantastic therapist who taught me the only person I need to trust is myself.

Here is how this works: When I listen to my intuition, my gut instinct, it leads me to safety. We are all designed this way. Some of us are more in tune with our intuition than others, but energy never lies. If something feels off, it likely is. Since learning this and how to set boundaries, I feel far more secure. Now, I am more trusting of others—I just know when to walk away.

A Recent Question Asked: Are there any good men left out there?

Many of us are divorced and started to date late in life. It can be daunting to get to know someone. You may go all in and get your heart broken. But, if you stay guarded, you may never know. So, it is important to remain vulnerable and open.

I would like to broaden the question to include women because it is a two-way street. Men and women feel the same way about wanting to find a loyal, respectful mate. So, let me address this in two parts.

Part one: if you feel there are no good people to date, perhaps you are looking in the wrong places. Consider that you need to work on yourself. For example, if you want a man (feel free to substitute a woman) who is financially successful, fit, funny, and loyal, you should also have those qualities. So, if you are sitting home on the couch unemployed, hoping to mooch off someone, not in shape, and have a record of cheating, you probably are not going to attract this dream person — like attracts like.

Part two: If you are with a man (or woman) who is not loyal or messes up, it may not be an indication that they are a "bad person," but instead, an indication of past trauma. This person may be self-sabotaging due to past trauma. If they are avoidant, for example, they may have a push-pull love style because they are terrified of rejection and abandonment.

Yes, there are plenty of eligible bachelors and bachelorettes, and the key is that we all do our self-work so that we do not carry baggage from past hurtful relationships or childhood and cause more wounds.

How to Rebuild Trust After Betrayal

Betrayal can take many forms, including affairs, addictions, hiding money, and stealing ideas at work, but the common thread is the breach of trust. Once trust has been broken, it is challenging to rebuild.

If you have been betrayed by your significant other, you have two choices: stay and repair the relationship or leave and rebuild your life. If you choose to stay, the following five steps will help you improve trust and boost a healthy, happy love connection.

Five Steps that Helped Me to Repair Trust in Relationships

1: A sincere apology with a promise to never repeat the action by the person who committed the betrayal.

2: Complete transparency on both people's parts. Access to phones, be where you say you are going to be, be on time, and return calls and texts.

3: Avoid rehashing details. The person who was betrayed can ask questions in the beginning to gain an understanding of what happened but avoid hurtful details. The *why* is far more critical in understanding and preventing it from happening again. Rehashing is like picking a scab and refusing to let the wound heal.

4: Be aware of changes in behavior. If your significant other suddenly stops returning texts and calls, starts sleeping on the couch, or works late and no longer joins you for dinner, they may repeat the destructive behavior.

5: Develop new rituals together as a couple. Take a daily walk or Friday night dinners out. Maybe we can start a new hobby together. This will help you bond and reconnect.

Final Thoughts

Reconnecting physically and emotionally with your significant other after betrayal is fundamental. This may seem counterintuitive, but something lacking led to the betrayal in the first place. Providing a safe, secure environment can help heal from past traumas and can even strengthen your relationship.

Once you commit to restoring the relationship, you must forgive your partner and work together without resentment and fear. Rehashing the betrayal will cause separation and scarcity and drive a wedge between you. If the betrayal continues, you will know there is a significant lack of respect, and your partner refuses to do the personal work and take responsibility. It is up to you to decide how much you are willing to tolerate.

If you are entering a new relationship, start very slowly with friendship. Get to know this person without disclosing all of the intimate details of your life immediately. Also, do not assume they are anything like your past relationships. Start with a fresh slate and give each person a fair chance. But you have the experience to recognize red flags. Have open conversations.

I wish you the best in restoring trust. Remember, trust yourself first and always.

"Trauma is not 'someone hurt my feelings.' It's a physical rewiring in the body that requires literal healing and rewiring—as literal as the healing required for a broken bone." ~Author Unknown

Setting Boundaries 101

Setting boundaries is essential in every relationship, including friends, co-workers, family members, neighbors, and romantic interests. Today, I will focus on romantic relationships. Whether you are dating or married, boundaries will help you set a foundation for a respectful, happy relationship. So, let's examine what that looks like, how to set them, and why so many people struggle with boundaries.

Seven Types of Boundaries I Feel Are Essential in Relationships

1. Personal Space Boundaries: Will you live together before marriage? Who will get what closet space? Where will you keep things organized?
2. Sexual Boundaries: Will you kiss in public? Are you kinky? How often will you have sex? Will you try new things?
3. Financial Boundaries: Will you share a bank account? Who will pay for what?
4. Intellectual Boundaries: What are your political views? Religious?
5. Emotional Boundaries
6. Time Boundaries- how much time you will spend together or apart.
7. Expectation Boundaries: What is your five-year plan? Long-term plan? Will you have children? How will you spend your holidays? How will you handle extended family?

Why Are Boundaries So Difficult for So Many People?

- Some never had to set them or even heard of them (I didn't

until I experienced a narcissistic relationship)
- Some are terrified of abandonment
- Others have acceptance issues

Examples of Boundaries in a Relationship

◇ I value your opinion, but this is my decision.

◇ I can text in the morning and evening, but I need to focus on work during the day, so if you text me and I do not reply, please do not feel hurt or like I don't love you. I am just focused on work during that time.

◇ I love spending time with you, but I also need a little time alone and some time for my friends and family.

Final Thoughts

Setting boundaries protects our emotional energy as well as our physical bodies. Set whatever boundary you feel you need. You can set new boundaries at any point in life. The key is to talk openly about your boundaries with your significant other so that you set them up for success.

If they break your boundaries, be firm and honest about how disappointing and hurtful that is to you. If they break it continuously, it is a sign of disrespect toward you — at that point, you need to evaluate if you want to remain in that toxic relationship.

"Love yourself enough to set boundaries. Your time and energy are precious. You get to choose how you use it. You teach people how to treat you by deciding what you will and won't accept." ~Anna Taylor

Soothing A Dysregulated Nervous System

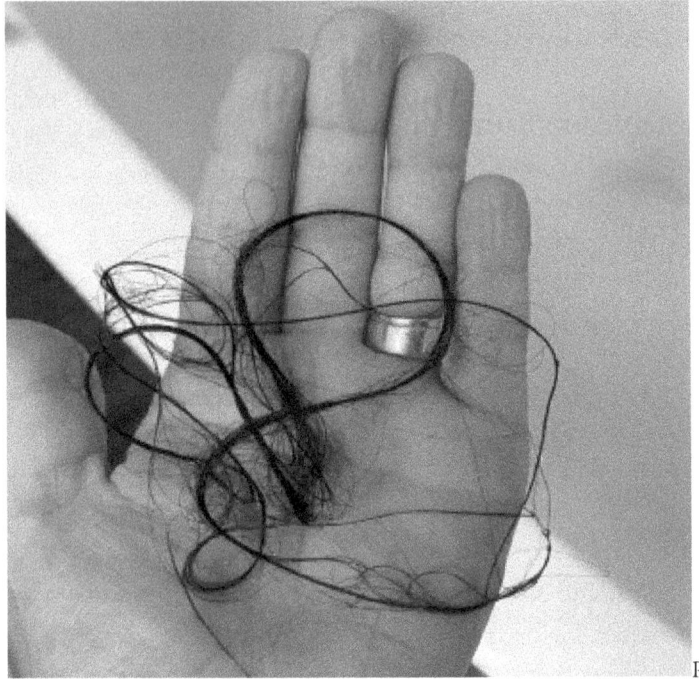

Image by Author
Personal

Living In Survival Mode

Are you constantly on the go or working on overdrive? Chronic stress or trauma can

cause us to become dysregulated. I have experienced psychological and physical abuse within the last three months, and my body is now showing physical symptoms. I have been losing clumps of hair, which is obviously unsettling, but it is one of the signs that my nervous system is dysregulated and likely a result of being unable to eat for some time, so I was malnourished. I wanted to write and discuss this critical topic with anyone else who might also be experiencing this.

The body and mind are interwoven. They signal each other when distressed. When stressed, our sympathetic nervous system is activated to keep us safe. Our heart rate
increases, our palms may become sweaty, and we may have difficulty concentrating. When we stay in this hypervigilant state too long, the nervous system cannot perform its roles efficiently.

When the sympathetic nervous system is activated, launching us into our fight-or-flight mode and the parasympathetic nervous system, AKA "the rest and digest," gets pushed aside, the body and mind become dysregulated and unbalanced.

Most people only experience the fight-or-flight mode in emergent situations for short periods. Unfortunately, those of us who have experienced more severe trauma live in more extensive survival mode, which is taxing to the nervous system and causes physical problems, stress, and anxiety.

Signs I Experienced of Nervous System Dysregulation

- Changes in appetite
- Overwhelm
- Irritability, reactiveness, being on edge
- Hair loss, chronic pain, skin rashes
- Insomnia, nightmares
- Memory problems, trouble recalling when put on the spot

Healing

Learn to recognize your triggers.

A trigger is anything that causes you to recall a painful emotional memory from an experience. It can be a place, a song, a smell, an argument... Recognize what upsets you. Triggers can be brutally painful, but they are messengers. Learn how to self-soothe rather than trying to avoid them.

Present moment awareness.

Become aware of your physical body. It will whisper hints. Listen to those clues that you are being triggered and that your sympathetic nervous system is being activated. When your heart starts racing, use deep breaths to immediately slow your heart rate back down, returning to the parasympathetic state.

Present-moment awareness helps remind us we are safe. Fear and worry come from past experiences and anxiety about the future. In the present, all is well. Look around and practice gratitude.

Feel it to heal it.

Feel each emotion as it surfaces. Observe it free from judgment. When we hold emotions down in our bodies, the energy becomes trapped and stagnant and can make us physically ill. Let the feelings flow through you. It may help to journal, and if you are struggling, it may help to talk with a trained professional.

Practice Self-Care

When regulating the nervous system, it is critical to practice good self-care. What exactly does that mean? It may sound basic, but the most basic tasks become a chore when you are dysregulated.

- Try to sleep well. Taking Magnesium Glycinate 400mg, three tablets per night helps me with my jumpy legs and helps relax me. You can also try melatonin or talk with your physician about other sleep supplements.
- Exercise-working out helps move energy through the body and reduces the body's stress hormones, such as adrenaline

and cortisone.
- Rest- literally take time to do nothing and do not feel guilty.
- Meditate.
- Spend time in nature.
- Laugh with friends. It can be easy to feel like having fun when experiencing tragedy is unnatural, but giving yourself permission to have fun is okay and healthy.
- Quiet your inner critic and be kind to yourself, and practice self-love.
- Practice positive affirmations.
- Do a creative project that boosts your self-esteem.

Final Thoughts

Talking about your thoughts and feelings might be helpful, but try not to ruminate. Process the trauma rather than continuously re-living it. Healing requires a higher level of self-awareness. We must learn our emotional triggers and how to self-soothe when our negative emotions become heightened to return to a balanced state more quickly.

The key to healing is the body-mind connection. It must maintain balance. The balance begins with awareness. Only each of us has the answers to what we need. Listen to your intuition. Practice self-study.

When you have experienced trauma and find yourself snapping at people, exhausted, having trouble sleeping, under or overeating, or unexplained rashes, those are all signs that your body is dysregulated. It is always a good idea to consult your physician anytime you have concerns. Many auto-immune diseases can emerge due to chronic stress and dysregulation of the nervous system, such as migraines, fibromyalgia, asthma, and gastrointestinal problems.

If you consult a physician, remember that you need to be your own advocate. Most doctors are trained for specific body parts rather than the nervous system itself. *The Dysautonomia Project* is a wonderful book that was given to me by a neurologist who was the first to explain this problem. He admitted that even though he lacked expert knowledge of the nervous system, I very much appreciated his referring me to the book. Seeing multiple specialists and being told there is nothing wrong with you can be very upsetting when you know there is — it is a form of medical gaslighting.

Remember, have faith in yourself, in your body and mind. You can heal yourself. Your hair will grow back if it is falling out like mine.

My rashes have gone away with better nutrition and vitamins. My appetite returned once my peace of mind was restored. Rest, peace, sunshine, grounding, and permission to slow down will restore your nervous system. Everything will be okay.

References:

Harvard Health Publishing Harvard Medical School Exercising to Relax , 2020 https://www.health.harvard.edu/staying-healthy/exercising-to-relax

Chelsea Long, MS, CSCS, TPI How the Parasympathetic Nervous System Can Lower Stress Hospital for Special Surgery, 2021

Kelly Freeman, David S. Goldstein, and Charles R. Thompson The Dysautonomia Project, 2015

"Every human has a true authentic self. Trauma is the disconnection from it, and healing is the reconnection to it." ~ Gabor Mate

Parting Words

What would you consider a deal breaker in your relationship?

A deal breaker is a bottom-line boundary with zero second chances. I would love to hear from you and know if you have a bottom line in place or have walked away from a previous relationship due to a broken bottom line. Do you believe you are or were in a relationship with a narcissist? You can reach out to me at contact@libbyshivelymcavoy.com anytime.

My deal breakers are lying and abuse of any kind, including emotional, psychological, verbal, sexual, financial, or physical, and I will not tolerate disrespect.

If you are newly out of a relationship with a narcissist, diagnosed, or highly suspected, please take your time recovering and connecting with yourself again. Jumping into another relationship may seem as if it would provide the comfort you want, but you are in a fragile state. It may take months before you realize how dysregulated your nervous system is. In fact, it took six months before all of my CPTSD symptoms fully surfaced.

When my nervous system finally calmed down—months after escaping my narcissist and going no contact, I started having regular bowel movements, my migraines went away, my hair stopped falling out, and my skin improved drastically. The body and mind are intricately connected. Be gentle with yourself. Practice good self-care, complete self-acceptance, and self-love. But also remember, grieving comes in waves, and that is exactly how your nervous system will cope with healing.

On days when you feel defeated, remember that they chose you because ***YOU ARE AMAZING***. They wanted someone who would make them look and feel good. No matter how many bad things they may say in their smear campaign, you both know it is not true.

Narcissists have a stunted and low level of emotional intelligence due to the trauma they endured as a child. When you fight with a narcissist, you might notice they act like a child. This is because whatever age the abuse occurred is when their emotional intelligence stopped developing.

Saying positive affirmations helps to rewire the subconscious mind, which is responsible for over ninety percent of our thoughts. The trick with positive affirmations is saying and repeating them often until we believe them. I like to write them in my journal as well as on sticky notes. I place the sticky notes on my bathroom mirror and the console of my car. This way I see them and repeat them throughout the day.

Examples of Positive Affirmations for Healing:

- I am worthy of love
- I am stronger than I realize
- I honor my emotions and give myself space to heal
- I let go of negative thoughts, hatred, and grudges and embrace a mindset of healing and positivity
- I prioritize my emotional and physical well-being
- I can do difficult things
- I am able to heal from the pain of the past

Lastly, I know it will be difficult for you to trust again. Learn to trust yourself above all else. Trust your intuition.

Affirmations for Trust

- I trust my gut instinct
- I trust my choices
- I am confident with my decisions
- My judgement is solid
- I trust the journey of life

Not every day will be good, but there is always something good in each day. Practice gratitude. Gratitude is the antidote to anxiety, fear, and hopelessness. Step outside and listen to the birds serenade you, put some relaxing music on, or light a candle. Remember, everything is temporary.

If you would like coaching I would be happy to connect with you and set up a plan for personal healing. https://LevelupwithLibbyPrivateCoaching.as.me/

You can also contact me here: contact@libbyshivelymcavoy.com

"I believe not only that trauma is curable, but that the healing process can be a catalyst for profound awakening." ~ Dr. Peter Levine

Gratitude

Thank you to all of my readers and my coaching clients. My purpose in life is to awaken, inspire, and empower you to step out of autopilot mode and live your best life, the life you are worthy of. I appreciate you all so much.

Thank you to my children, who, unfortunately, were exposed to my narcissistic ex. I know you watched me go through hell. I am sorry I scared you. I am not proud of the person I became while with that man, but I am super proud of my comeback. Remember, the comeback is always stronger than the setback. I love you both and I am so proud of you.

To my family and friends: thank you. You know who you are, and you know I love you. You inspire me so much and help me stay positive and healthy. Extra big hugs in appreciation of your support.

Finally, thank you, Dr. Gabriella Korosi, for editing and publishing this book with Dancing Elephants Press. I appreciate all the hard work you put into this entire process. You are not only a publisher but an amazing woman and wonderful friend. I am honored to have a portion of this book support the elephant sanctuary.

Previously published books by Libby Shively McAvoy and Dancing Elephants Press Include

Holistic Journey Toward Wellness – December 2022
   An amazing collection of stories about health and wellness written by 21 authors from all over the world. 560 pages of knowledge shared through lived experiences and wisdom. A true treasure. Available online and in print format.

The Magic In Friendship – February 2024
   There have never been two friends that were exactly like or equal to any two other friends. It's a special bond and relationship that is always evolving and yet stays the same because of the relationship as a friend. No matter the time or distance, as demonstrated within, the message of love, friendship, trust, and safety is on display within the pages. The faces of friendship are presented and examined. At the conclusion of this book, you will walk away with an idea of how to be a friend, make all types of friends, and maintain their friendship regardless of distance or time. Friendship is key to being a well-rounded person. Learn from these women and the people they have shared their friendship with over the years.
   Rated G for great, F for fun, and S to help you improve your own spirituality. In case you're wondering, these women are also my friends.
   DR Rawson

Creative Writing Ideas to Spark Your Imagination - December 2023
   52 writing prompts created by Dancing Elephants Press Editors. "Prompts are everywhere and are in everything. It comes in different names too. Signals, intuition, gut feelings, fear etc., depending on your circumstance and or situation in life. A writing Prompt sparks creativity sending many signals to the brain. It possesses the power to ignite innovation, expand imagination, and send your brain into places you can't imagine naturally. It will tickle your funny bone; you can't believe that you wrote that hilarious story. It also teaches the writer new and amazing things about themselves. Dancing Elephant Press have added a new color, flavor, taste, style, feeling, and excitement to prompts and how amazing they are with their 52 Week prompts." by Annelise Lords

101 Universal Messages – November 2023
   100 poems and 1 call to action. Poetry by Gabriella. 30 years of poetry in one magical little book. 151 pages in this poetry book you will find poems dedicated to people passed on, poems of inspiration and joy, love, healing and nature. Poems that are playful and sad. A wide variety like life.

Moments of Eternity – August 2023
Written by 15 beautiful poets from all corners of the world. A collection of amazing poems that bring a beautiful variety of light, joy, and inspiration into our lives. 292 pages of joyful poetry and inspiration.

The Joy of Life - July 2023
Written by 11 amazing authors from all over the world, it is an essay collection of personal experiences about spirituality, inspiration, and joy.

Darkness and Light – March 2022
Story collections by Dr. Gabriella Kőrösi from 2021 where you find anything from recipes to inspiration, motivation, health, grief, human suffering, writing, travel and fun stories.

Bringing the light into your life 2022
The goal of this mediation bundle is to provide calmness, healing, love, happiness, bringing light and joy into your life. Including 6 meditations, introductory and closing articles. The book includes an introductory article about unity and harmony. Meditations: Lift Your Spirits Up — Bringing Love and Joy into Your Life, Centering Yourself in Unconditional Love, Healing Meditation - Love Energy Transition, Opening Your Heart and Letting your Fears Go, Universal Love Meditation, Providing Energy Protection and Perfect Moments.

Limitless New Beginnings – 2022 - short story booklet
This story is about past, present, and future. It is a fiction, yet it is not. A version of this story was published in a short story book for children If I Could Be by Dr. Gabriella Kőrösi. This is the original adult version of the story. The story about beginnings, struggles and beginnings again. The main character is Little Rose who is been reborn after centuries.. The story shows her past, preset and future.

If I could be Poetry and Short Story book – 2021
This poem inspired some of the poems written in this book by other poets.
If I Could be is one of my favorite poems I wrote. The book contains multiple poems; some poems are in multiple languages. Mostly English and Hungarian. If I could be had been translated into French, Nigerian -Igbo as well as Spanish. My goal with this book was to create joy and spark the imagination. The book is created for all ages. The book has young artists and their drawings, paintings as well as pictures of the artist who created the drawings and paintings. The book has 20 poems and 3 fun short stories. The short stories include a Bee story when bees moved into our house; a story about new beginnings and my personal favorite the story about the time when my son and I had a road trip, and I lost my pants in Texas. I hope you will enjoy this

short story poem book. All the poems and short stories are fun and uplifting. The idea was to create something joyful in this difficult time during the pandemic.

Our Society: Addiction and More Uncovered in 2020

This book tells the stories and personal experiences of professionals from the addiction field as well as individuals, their friends, and families who had experienced addiction in their lives. The book covers stories from over 50 individuals. Addiction Uncovered looks at addiction more than a disease. It touches the soul through stories told from multiple viewpoints. It shows the individual who experienced addiction, a family member who lived with someone who previously had or currently has addiction. Additionally, stories from nurses, doctors, social workers, teachers and more. I hope you will enjoy this book and pass on the stories to others.